THE
TECHNICAL
REHEARSAL

A COMEDY

Alan Marshall

Published by Playstage
United Kingdom.

An imprint of Write Publications Ltd

www.playsforadults.com

Designed by Kate Lowe, Greensands Graphics
Printed by Creeds Ltd, Bridport, Dorset

Note to producers about performing "The Technical Rehearsal"

The Set

The action takes place in a village hall or small theatre, a few days before the first night of a production of *Cinderella*, so the set is partially built and painted. During the action of the play, a line of flats have to be moved forward slightly and, therefore, it is suggested that the flats are screwed to each other, held up by stage weights, but are not attached in any way to the back wall or sides of the stage.

The area in front of the stage is essential to the action and it is therefore necessary that your venue has an exit/entrance to the front or side of the stage that the actors can use as an alternative to going across the stage. The lighting and sound controls have to be operated (or *seen* to be operated) from a table in front of the stage.

A major part of the action at the end of Act 1 is the raising of the cut-out Cinderella coach by means of a rope. It goes without saying that the cut-out coach must be made of very light materials but the actors must, by a process of mime, make it appear to be very heavy. The coach is dropped from the ceiling during a blackout and, therefore, safety must be of paramount importance during the production. For this event, all actors must be well clear of the area where the coach will fall. You will see in the text that the coach should end up on its front, covering the pumpkin. This should be done by the man at the side lowering the coach to the floor and, in the blackout, someone gently pushing the coach forward to rest face down.

The pumpkin "goo" can be achieved by one of the actors having a bucket of the goo just offstage and, in the blackout, smearing it on to "DEBBIE".

Obviously, the above should be carefully rehearsed many times before actual performance.

Plotting the moves

The whole point of this play is that it is simulated reality. The audience is supposed to be spying on a real technical rehearsal. Therefore you cannot have any actors standing idle. There are instructions in the text for mimes/tasks for the actors which take place while a main conversation is happening. These mimes have to be subtle, so that they give the impression of people being occupied but they do not detract from the actors who are speaking.

THE TECHNICAL REHEARSAL

CAST *(In order of appearance)*

PETER	set builder, meticulous and obstinate, age 60+
PATSY	producer, frayed at the edges, age 40+
JOAN	actor, playing Stepmother, likes 'stirring' things, age 50+
VAL	stage manager, married to Roger, age 60+
SHIRLEY	Peter's wife and unofficial tea lady, age 60+
JOHN	actor playing Prince Charming, approaching 40 and concerned
DEBBIE	actor playing Cinderella, neurotic, lots of allergies, age 35+
ERIC	unflappable sound and lighting man, any age
ROGER	actor, playing one of the Ugly Sisters, age 60+
NORMAN	actor, playing one of the Ugly Sisters, jokey, also serial adulterer, age 50+
BARBARA	assistant stage manager, slightly formidable, married to Roy, age 60+
RENEE	actor playing the Fairy Godmother, age 60+
LINDA	prompt, married to Ron, age 40+
JOE	actor, playing Buttons, harassed and persistent financial services salesman, age 40+
ROY	actor, playing Baron Hardup, hen-pecked husband of Barbara, age 60+
ELLIE	actor, eager teenager, desperate for a part
RON	actor, playing Dandini, also society's publicity officer, computer geek, age 40+
SHARON	former member of the society, now Norman's secret mistress, age 40+
MORRY	actor, playing The Chamberlain, 'jack the lad', always laughing, age 50+
SONJA	Morry's wife, 'the life and soul of the party', age 50+
JEAN	Norman's long-suffering wife about to exact revenge, age 40+

9 males and 11 females.
The action takes place in a village hall, on and in front of the stage.

THE TECHNICAL REHEARSAL
ACT I

The area in front of the stage is part of the action. The stage itself is partially set as a medieval street scene with a cottage stage right with, woodland in the background and then a palace stage left. The set gives the impression of being incomplete. The palace has an archway. There is a large pair of stepladders by the archway. No stage furniture or props as yet. The lighting table is to the side and in front of the stage. It can be seen by the audience and is part of the action but it does not impede their view. There are some steps leading up to the front of the stage. As the lights come up, PATSY is sitting on the front of the stage looking fed up and PETER is climbing up the ladder with his tools to do something to the top of the archway. Neither is speaking to each other. JOAN enters through the side door.

JOAN	Hi Patsy!.*(stopping and looking at the set)* Oh! I thought……..
PATSY	*(depressed)* I know. Don't say anything please.
PETER	*(calling out but not turning round)* I followed the plan exactly. I did exactly as I was told.
JOAN	Oh.
PATSY	*(desperately)* If only I'd been here this afternoon, Joan, but I had to go to the kid's sports day. I couldn't get out of it.
JOAN	No, of course you couldn't. What are you going to do?
PATSY	We'll just have to change all the moves.
JOAN	Oh God.

PATSY	I know.
JOAN	It's going to be a bit awkward having the archway on that side of the stage isn't it?
PETER	*(calling out again, without turning round)* Don't blame me. I just followed the plan.
PATSY	*(getting ratty)* Peter, why would I rehearse everyone coming in through an archway upstage right if I had drawn a plan where the archway was upstage left?
PETER	It *is* upstage right.
JOAN	No Peter. You've put the archway upstage left.
PETER	*(not turning round but sticking out his right hand)* Can't you tell your right from your left? This is right.
PATSY	*(sighing) To* the *audience* it's right, but *not* to the actors – how long have you been doing amateur dramatics? Anyway, the plan showed the archway over here. What did you do, hold it up to a mirror while you worked?
PETER	*(defensively)* It wasn't just me. Joe and Roger and Norman were helping me and they didn't say anything.
JOAN	*(dryly)* Case of the blind leading the blind I would think.
PATSY	You never said a truer word. But, that's not the half of it. Peter's built Cinderella's coach, haven't you Peter?
PETER	*(defensively)* I hope you're not going to criticise that coach. It took me and my son-in-law three weeks to build that.
PATSY	*(sarcastically)* It's a wonderful coach. Or it would be for the London Palladium, but we can't get it on the stage now. The point of having the archway there was so that we could get it through the back door and onto the stage

without any obstructions. You've now put a flat there and all the cast have got to sidle along the back wall to get onstage. We certainly couldn't get the coach onstage now. Anyway, it's too heavy to lift.

JOAN   Really?

PATSY   Oh yes.

JOAN   But the fairies were supposed to bring it on. Peter, you knew that four little girls had to bring it on.

PETER   I like to do a job properly but suddenly that's a crime. *(He stomps off on a huff.)*

JOAN   Oh God. This is a terrible start.

PATSY   There's more.

JOAN   Surely not?

PATSY   Oh yes. Ann phoned me up this morning. The fairies had a hockey match on Friday and Rebecca has broken her leg, so we're down to three fairies, and Ann forgot to tell me that they were all on a Guide's camping trip this weekend and they're not coming back until late tonight, so they can't make the technical rehearsal. I mean, how could she just forget? She knows how important technical rehearsals are.

(VAL enters with a box full of props)

JOAN   Look at the set, Val.

VAL   I know. Roger came home and told me. I was going to ring you but I didn't think you would be going home after the sports day.

PATSY   Roger told you? So he *knew* it was wrong?

VAL   Yes. But apparently none of the others could persuade Peter it was wrong. Norman went home in disgust actually.

PATSY   Well that was helpful of him. I'm not sure what annoys me more – Peter's obstinacy or the other three's lack of backbone.

JOAN   You just can't leave them unsupervised for a minute can you?

VAL   I've got the fairy dust by the way. I went into town and bought loads of tubes of glitter. We can try it out tonight can't we?

JOAN   I don't think so. We won't have any fairies.

VAL   Oh you're joking!

PATSY   And when we *do* get them, we'll only have three. And they won't be able to lift the coach onstage.

VAL   What?!

JOAN   It's too big and heavy apparently and the archway's in the wrong place.

PATSY   Go and have a look at it. It's out the back.

(VAL and JOAN exit. PATSY sits still. SHIRLEY comes in with a cup of tea.)

SHIRLEY   Peter's ever so upset Patsy. He thinks you're not speaking to him.

(She hands over the cup of tea)

PATSY   Thank you. For the moment he'd be right. I'm sorry, Shirley, but I can't think what possessed your husband to build the set like this. It's caused all sorts of problems.

SHIRLEY   I think he realises but I'm afraid he finds it ever so difficult to apologise. He always has.

PATSY	Huh. Him and the rest of the male population!
SHIRLEY	He's worked ever so hard on this set, Patsy. He really has.
PATSY	I know he has, Shirley. And I expect I will eventually forgive him. But just at the moment I've got rather a lot of problems to sort out before we put this pantomime on.
SHIRLEY	I know. Would you like some paracetomol?
PATSY	Yes I would actually. Thanks.
SHIRLEY	I've got some in my bag.
	(SHIRLEY exits. JOAN and VAL come back in)
JOAN	It's incredible! I've never seen anything like it! I mean it's a fabulous coach but it's enormous!
VAL	Ssh! Shirley will hear you.
PATSY	I think Shirley is all too aware that Peter blotted his copybook. She just been in and sort-of apologised to me.
	(SHIRLEY comes back in with two paracetomol tablets)
SHIRLEY	There you are.
	(JOHN and DEBBIE arrive, carrying costumes. They stop and gawp at the set.)
DEBBIE	I'm sorry we're late. John gave me a lift but I forgot my inhaler and we had to go back for it. *(She sees the set)* Oh no. We just met Norman in the car park. He said there were problems.
SHIRLEY	I'm just going to fill the urn up. *(She exits)*
VAL	Shirley's embarrassed because Peter's messed the set up.
JOHN	You and your big mouth, Debbie.
DEBBIE	I can't help it. These new antihistamine's I'm taking make

me a bit spaced out.

JOHN I'm glad I wasn't here today otherwise *I* would have been blamed for the set.

VAL Yes, well, Patsy's not too happy with Roger, Joe and Norman, I can tell you.

PATSY No I'm not.

JOHN *(getting up on the stage and looking through the archway)* Bloody hell. There's not much room back here.

(ERIC, the electrician, enters with bags.)

ERIC Jesus Christ! What happened?

PATSY Eric, I haven't got the strength to tell everyone individually. Can you wait until everyone's here, then I will make an announcement.

ERIC Fair enough – but you do realise that I am going to have to move half the lights now.

(ERIC goes and sits at the lighting table.)

PATSY Of course I do. It's going to be a long night. *(As she is speaking, NORMAN and ROGER come in. They look anxious. NORMAN is wearing an expensive multi-coloured sweater.)* *(PATSY is sarcastic)* Oh, look. If it isn't the Cashmere King and his sidekick! Another new jumper I see, Norman. I suppose the two of you have come to admire your handiwork have you?

ROGER We did tell him.

NORMAN I couldn't take any more and I went home. It was farcical.

PATSY I find it amazing that you three couldn't make him understand. Where is the other musketeer by the way?

NORMAN	Joe had some sales meeting this afternoon. He left at lunchtime.
ROGER	We were just here as labourers. Peter just sort of blinded us with technical terms.
PATSY	*(withering)* What like "hammer" and "nails"? What's technical about putting flats up in the right order, Roger? We've been rehearsing this for three months and we have all understood that the archway goes in front of the backstage door, haven't we ladies?
	(The women all nod and murmur 'yes'.)
NORMAN	*(putting his arm around PATSY and attempting to be jokey)* Oh yeah but we're only men, Patsy. You can't expect us to get it right can you?
ROGER	Yeah. And she wasn't here, was she, Norman? You can't expect us to get it right if you're not here to tell us.
PATSY	Well, you're the ones who are going to suffer because you are going to have to redo all your moves tonight. I hope you don't expect to be home before midnight.
NORMAN	Oh blige. I'd better make a phone call. *(He makes for the door.)*
DEBBIE	*(meeting NORMAN as she comes in and he goes out. She has a wig in her hand)* Oh hello Norman. Is that another new jumper?
NORMAN	Of course. *(He goes to put his arm round her in a greeting.)*
DEBBIE	No! Don't get near me. Cashmere always makes me sneeze.
NORMAN	No it can't , surely? Top quality stuff cashmere. You can't be allergic to that.

DEBBIE   Well I am. It's all the very fine hair. *(NORMAN shrugs and exits)* Patsy, this wig that I'm supposed to put on when I get done up for the ball – it looks horrible. My mum tried everything with it but it just doesn't work. Can I put it on and show you?

PATSY   OK. But put it on with the ballgown so I can see the whole effect.

DEBBIE   OK. My mum had to wash it three times before I could get anywhere near it. It gave me terrible headaches.

JOAN   Why?

DEBBIE   It must have had mould spores in it. The minute I took it out of the plastic bag I started getting a sinus reaction.

JOHN   Do you want us all in costume tonight?

PATSY   I do really because I want to see if the colours look OK.

ROGER   Make up?

PATSY   Well I think you and Norman definitely. But don't take too long because we have a lot of work to do.

ROGER   Right.

              (DEBBIE, JOHN, ROGER and JOAN exit by going up on to the stage and going through the archway. We can see that there is not much room for them to get behind the flats. JOHN goes first and the others pass costumes to ROGER who then passes them to JOHN behind the flats. JOAN and DEBBIE peer round the back of the flats and then turn to speak to PATSY.)

JOAN   I am never going to get behind this set with my costume on. Neither will Debbie.

DEBBIE	I'm going to get claustrophobic if I have to go behind here.
PATSY	You're only there for thirty seconds.
DEBBIE	It doesn't matter. I can't be closed in for any length of time.
JOAN	Oh dear.
PATSY	Oh it's no good. I'll have to get Peter to change some things. If he's back there can you ask him to come and see me? Thanks.
VAL	I'll go and see if he's down in the cellar. (*VAL exits.*)
DEBBIE	I'll have to go round the front way for the moment. *(She comes off the stage and exits through the door.)*
JOAN	I think she gets worse when she's under stress.
PATSY	She's only been here five minutes and we've had three ailments already.
JOAN	She's brought her own make-up.
PATSY	Why?
JOAN	Apparently our make-up brings her out in a rash.
	(*JOAN exits behind the set. JOHN re-appears from behind the set.*)
JOHN	Patsy. Can I just talk to you about something?
PATSY	Sure.
JOHN	It's this business of kissing Debbie….
PATSY	Oh look. I've let you skip it during rehearsals because I know you find it embarrassing but Prince Charming has got to kiss Cinderella at the end of the panto. You can't get out of it.
JOHN	It's not that I find it embarrassing – well I do – but – it's –

	well – *(lowering his voice)* I don't want to catch anything off her.
PATSY	She's not ill – you know – disease, ill – she's just got allergies and things. You can't catch those from a little peck on the lips.
JOHN	How do you know she hasn't got some disease? I mean, how can you tell? She's got so many things wrong with her.
PATSY	Look. Trust me. She hasn't got an infectious disease. Just give her a quick peck and hold your breath. OK? *(JOHN exits looking doubtful and PATSY goes over to the lighting table)* I'd just like to go through the tricky bits in Act One before you adjust any of the lights. Can you wait until the tea break?
ERIC	Sure. It won't take long. What a lash up!
PATSY	I hate technical rehearsals. By the way, the fairies won't be here tonight but we'll go through the sound and light bits anyway.
ERIC	Where are they then?
PATSY	Guide camp. Ann forgot to tell me. And we're down to three because one of them broke her leg at a hockey match. All we need is for the other three to get food poisoning round the campfire and we're right up the creek without a paddle.
ERIC	You'll have to dress Val and Shirley up as fairies. I'd love that.
	(VAL enters)
PATSY	*(laughing)* Here, Val, Eric thinks you should learn the

fairies' lines in case the girls don't come back from
guide camp.

VAL   *(not amused)* Ha, ha.

(BARBARA enters)

ERIC   Watch out. Here comes another one!

(PATSY and ERIC laugh).

BARBARA   What's he saying?

VAL   He's being rude about us, Barbara. He says we have to
understudy the fairies in case they don't come back from
Guide camp.

BARBARA   Oh I'm game. I don't think I've ever played a fairy but I'll
give it a go. Trouble is, we'd all be older than the fairy
godmother.

ERIC   Only just.

PATSY   Cor, you've got a death wish tonight. Renee will have your
guts for garters when she hears.

*(RENEE appears onstage, from behind the set, dressed as
the fairy godmother with a broken wand. Everyone starts
laughing.)*

RENEE   See? This is just the reaction the audience is going to have.
You should have made Joan the fairy godmother. She
would have been more dignified.

BARBARA   Don't be silly. It's only 'cos your wand is broken. Give it to
me and I'll see if I can repair it.

(BARBARA exits with the broken wand.)

VAL   You look lovely.

RENEE	Can you see my vest?
PATSY	Oh Renee, you haven't got a vest on have you?
RENEE	It's very cold out there.
VAL	One of the heaters has packed up. I wondered if Eric could have a look at it. Everyone's complaining about the cold.
ERIC	I suppose so. God! All these frail little women!
RENEE	*(firmly)* I am *not* frail and it *is* cold.
ERIC	Alright, alright.
	(ERIC exits and VAL follows. NORMAN appears from behind the set, briefly, just wearing a pair of trousers. His chest is bare and he is carrying his carefully folded cashmere jumper.)
RENEE	Well you obviously don't find the dressing room too cold Norman.
NORMAN	What me? I'm hot-blooded Renee…you should know that by now. Has anyone seen my padded hanger?
PATSY	No. There's a coat hanger here. *(She picks up a wire coat hanger from near the stage.)*
NORMAN	Ooh no. You can't hang cashmere on a wire coat hanger. It will go all out of shape.
PATSY	Sorry Norman. I haven't seen it. Try looking in the cloakroom.
NORMAN	I brought that hanger in especially last week. I wish people would leave my things alone. *(He exits.)*
RENEE	Him and his expensive jumpers. Shall I go and put the urn on?

PATSY	Shirley's already done it I think.
	(LINDA enters.)
LINDA	Shall I go home and get a bottle of wine? Or would Prozac help.
PATSY	You've seen it then.
LINDA	Yes. I was thinking about booking it for the next WI trip.
RENEE	What's she talking about?
PATSY	Cinderella's coach. Haven't you seen it?
LINDA	You can hardly miss it. It's right in front of the entrance.
RENEE	Oh, I came in the back way. Is it a sight, Linda?
LINDA	It's magnificent. Large enough to take a football team to Wembley in I should think. Ron will be along in a minute. He's just playing with his new computer. *(As an afterthought to RENEE)* By the way, you do look a very forlorn fairy.
RENEE	Thank you Linda. I think I just about represent the spirit of this show. One forlorn fairy of pensionable age.
	(RENEE exits upstage in a huff.)
PATSY	*(to LINDA)* I think you'd better go and get *her* the Prozac.
	(NORMAN and ROGER attempt to come on stage, in costume, from behind the flats but NORMAN clowns about and bangs on the flats shouting.)
NORMAN's VOICE	Shouldn't there be an archway here?
ROGER's VOICE	Excuse me Madam Producer but we can't get on the stage!

PATSY	Very funny. I don't know what you're laughing about. (*To LINDA*) They're a pair of sods aren't they?
ERIC	*(entering and making for his lighting table)* Who are you talking about?
NORMAN'S VOICE	Actually, Patsy, we seriously can't get on to the stage in these costumes.
PATSY	Those two.
ROGER'S VOICE	No, it's just too small dear.
NORMAN'S VOICE	We don't want to hear about your personal problem, Roger – I'm trying to tell Patsy that there's not enough room behind the flats.
PATSY	*(shouting back)* I'm waiting for Peter. Have you seen him?
NORMAN'S VOICE	Yes. He's here.
PATSY	*(shouting again)* Could you ask him to come round the front please? *(In a normal voice to LINDA)* I asked Peter to come and see me ages ago. I suppose he's sulking.
LINDA	The thing you have to remember is that people are just doing their best . It's their hobby. You can't expect too much of them.
PATSY	Oh I know. Stop being so nice – it makes me feel guilty.
LINDA	Oh don't feel guilty. Just punch him in the face then you'll feel better.
	(PETER enters looking tense.)

PATSY   *(trying to pretend that there isn't a problem)* Peter, the actors are having trouble getting out onstage in their costumes. Do you think that we could just shift the flats along the back forward a bit to give them some more room?

PETER   *(also trying to pretend that there isn't a problem)* I should think so. I'll have to unscrew the supports at the top. I'll have a look in the cellar to see if there are some longer bits of wood.

(PETER exits)

LINDA   *(getting a chair and sitting down with her script, ready to prompt)* You handled that very well dear.

PATSY   Oh yes. I'm good at massaging egos.

(NORMAN and ROGER appear through the door in front of the stage dressed as the Ugly Sisters with lots of badly done make-up on.)

LINDA   Oh look, it's the Spice Girls.

(Everyone laughs and NORMAN does a rendition of "I tell you what I want, what I really really want..." BARBARA enters while he is doing this.)

BARBARA   That's really good, you should keep that in.

NORMAN   I always said you were good at spotting talent, Barbara.

PATSY   Don't encourage them. The pair of them are ad-libbing enough as it is. It's really throwing Debbie. Seriously, you two, can you cut down on the ad-libbing when you've got a scene with Debbie? She's having enough trouble with her lines as it is.

ROGER	Of course we will dear.
PATSY	Is Debbie ready yet? She wanted to show me her wig and costume.
BARBARA	No, she's in the toilet. Bit of a funny tummy I think. She's been in there for ages.
PATSY	Oh crumbs.
BARBARA	By the way, I've seen the coach. It's incredible. What are you going to do with it?
PATSY	Just at this moment, Barbara, I have no idea. Is everybody else in costume, only I'd like to see them on stage?
BARBARA	I think so – except for Joe and Morry - they're not here yet. *(BARBARA sits down on one side of the stage, gets out a sewing kit and starts to repair the bottom of the stage curtains. She has the repaired wand with her.)*
LINDA	Ron said he would change at home before he came out.
PATSY	Morry and Sonja only got back from Spain today but he said he would get here as soon as he could. Where's Joe? *(As she says that JOE rushes in, completely dressed in his costume as Buttons)*
JOE	*(not in a good mood)* I'm here, I'm here. I've just driven back from Surrey.
NORMAN	What like that?
JOE	Well I had to. I haven't had time to go home. I had a sales meeting.
ROGER	On a Sunday?
JOE	It's the only time we could all get together. The company's got problems.

PATSY	I thought you worked for yourself?
JOE	I am a self-employed financial consultant but I work as part of a big organisation. That's what we had the meeting about. They want us to sell more Patsy, they always do.
PATSY	Oh.

(Everyone else files in through the door. RENEE is the Fairy Godmother, JOHN is Prince Charming, ROY is Cinderella's father, Baron Hardup, JOAN is the stepmother, Baroness Hardup.)

PATSY	Can I see you all up on the stage please?

(They all go up on the stage.)

BARBARA	Oh, I've mended your wand dear. *(hands it to RENEE and turns to PATSY)* Do you want me to go and see if Debbie's alright?
JOAN	It's OK. She's out of the loo now. She'll be here in a moment.

(DEBBIE comes in with her ballgown costume and wig on)

DEBBIE	Sorry, my irritable bowel syndrome always flares up when I'm stressed. What do you think of the wig?
PATSY	It's alright actually. The whole outfit looks fine. Have you got your other costume on underneath it?
DEBBIE	Yes. But it's very itchy. I just hope it doesn't make my eczema worse.

(VAL enters.)

PATSY	Have you practised getting that frock on Debbie quickly?
VAL	Well not really. She's been in the loo all this time.

(ELLIE enters, carrying a bag, goes up to PATSY and hovers eagerly, waiting for a pause in the conversation)

DEBBIE   Sorry.

PATSY   No, it's OK. That's what this evening is supposed to be for – practising the quick costume changes.

VAL   It's going to be difficult to practise that whole bit without any fairies here.

PATSY   I know, I know. We're going to have to have another technical tomorrow night.

(A mobile phone rings. Everyone has left their bags in front of the stage. DEBBIE dives off the stage to her bag, JOE dives off the stage to his bag, ERIC stands up and takes his mobile out of his pocket and ELLIE takes her mobile out of her bag. Everyone except JOE puts their mobile back and resumes their places.)

PATSY   Oh no. The mobiles have started early tonight.

JOE   Hallo? Just a minute. *(Speaks to PATSY)* I have to keep mine on – I'm expecting an important client to ring me. *(Goes outside with his phone)* Sorry, what were you saying....

DEBBIE   As soon as my reflexologist rings back with my next appointment, I'll switch mine off. But I've been trying to get hold of her all day. I've got to have my energy lines boosted.

ERIC   I'm on call – I did warn you.

ELLIE   Sorry I'm late. I'll switch my mobile off.

PATSY   That's OK dear.

ELLIE	I heard you say there were no fairies. I can be a fairy for tonight.
PATSY	Actually you can be a fairy every night, Ellie, because Rebecca has broken her leg.
ELLIE	*(ecstatic)* Great! No, sorry, I didn't mean great...for Rebecca.. I meant...
PATSY	Yes I know.
VAL	She'll be bigger than the other fairies.
PATSY	True.
JOAN	Well can't she be a chief fairy or something?
PATSY	It's the costume that's the problem.
ELLIE	My mum will make one tomorrow.
RENEE	I don't think your mum could manage to make a fairy costume that quickly.
ELLIE	Yes she can. She can alter one of my dance costumes.
PATSY	Good, well that's settled then.
NORMAN	If we're doing another technical tomorrow, does that mean we're not going to have Wednesday off?
PATSY	I don't think so, do you?
	(Everyone groans.)
ROGER	I did say dear, when we started – one of my conditions was that I couldn't make Wednesday nights because of my evening class.
PATSY	I know, but this is an emergency, isn't it!
ROGER	I know but...

JOAN I was supposed to be going out to dinner at my son's on Wednesday night.

DEBBIE I was going to go to my chiropractor and get my back done.

PATSY *(losing her temper finally and shouting)* And I was looking forward to having a night off from all the bloody aggravation caused by this whole damn production! We can't all have what we want can we? I would have liked a set that was exactly as I planned it but I can't! I would like to have actors who know their bloody lines but I can't! In fact, after this production, I would like to have my goddamn life back! I would like to have a few months of my life not looking at a bunch of people who stand around like sheep waiting for a border collie to arrive!

(She storms out, bumping into PETER in the doorway, who is entering with an armful of pieces of wood. Everyone shuffles around on the stage looking awkward and making faces at each other.)

PETER *(unaware of what has happened – shouts)* Shirley! *(SHIRLEY appears from the kitchen.)* Make us all a cup of tea girl, will you? They might as well have a cuppa while I move the set.

SHIRLEY Right. *(SHIRLEY exits. People drift down from the stage. PETER moves the ladders and starts unscrewing the supports attached to the wall.)*

NORMAN Well, that told us didn't it?

LINDA I'll go and see if she's alright. *(LINDA exits and JOE returns.)*

JOAN I can understand how she feels.

JOHN	She hasn't lost her temper like that before.
NORMAN	No. *(Attempting a joke)* I mean if you wanted that sort of display of temper you could stay at home couldn't you?
PETER	What happened?
DEBBIE	Patsy got very upset.
PETER	It's probably her hormones.
	(All the women go "Oh!" or "tut".)
RENEE	What a disgraceful thing to say.
VAL	Men! You're all the same!
ROGER	Well thank you Peter. Now you've turned them *all* against us!
RENEE	Why is it that when men lose their temper it's because they've been justly provoked and when women lose their temper it must be because their hormones are playing up?
JOE	I dunno. But that's the way it always is.
RENEE	Do you really believe that?
JOE	Renee, I just do as I'm told. I am a man and therefore not capable of intelligent thought.
BARBARA	Of course you're not. Roy! Go and change your shoes, they look daft.
ROY	Yes dear.
	(ROY exits. SHIRLEY arrives with the tea. Everyone murmurs "Lovely" "Thank you Shirley" and so on. RON arrives with a pile of newsletters and carrying a bag with more paper stuff in. He is dressed as Dandini.)
RON	Hello everyone! Oh, tea already?
JOAN	*(taking him to one side)* Just to put you in the picture, Ron

- Peter built the set wrongly, one fairy has broken her leg, the others are at Guide Camp and can't come tonight, so Patsy has called for another technical rehearsal tomorrow, the actors, as usual, are being difficult, and Patsy got upset and stormed off.

RON   Is she coming back!?

JOAN   Oh yes. At least I hope so. I'm sure she just needed to have some time on her own for a moment. Linda's gone to find her. Patsy wouldn't desert us.

RON   No – 'course she wouldn't. *(Calling out)* I've got this month's newsletter everyone! I think you're going to be pleasantly surprised. *(He starts to hand them out.)*

RENEE   Oh look! Coloured photos!

JOHN   Wow! It looks like my company magazine!

ROGER   How did you do it Ron? I mean this is the best yet.

RON   Well I upgraded my system. I've now got a colour scanner and new software. I can do anything now. In fact, I've got some samples of special Christmas cards. I thought I might sell them and raise some money for us.

             (RON gets out four sample Christmas cards and lays them on the stage.)

VAL   Oh look! They've got the group name on!

RENEE   And the date! Oh Ron, you are clever!

RON   I can even put your name and address inside with the greeting if you want.

NORMAN   That's a really good idea. How much are you going to charge then?

RON	(*producing another piece of paper*) Well, I've drawn up a price list based on number of sheets of card, the cost of my printer cartridges and the price of envelopes.
JOE	That's a good price for envelopes. Where did you get this Ron?
RON	Actually, I've got Broadband now and I just went on the Net and trawled through a few stationery suppliers.
ROGER	Oh, you've got Broadband now? My word. All this hi-tech wizardry. It's beyond me.
JOE	Yeah. But you have to keep up with the times Roger. Nowadays no-one can do without it, either through a pc or through the television. Especially now digital TV has come in.
ROGER	Television?
NORMAN	Oh yes. My brother's doing that.
ROGER	What, going on the Internet through the telly? How does that work then?
NORMAN	I don't know. How does that work then Ron?
JOE	Forget about surfing the Web through the telly. Doing it with your mobile phone is *the* thing.
ROGER	Doing it with your mobile phone?
NORMAN	(*giggling*) Would you care to rephrase that!
JOE	Oh yeah. You just dial up the number and bingo.
ROGER	You can't get much on a mobile phone screen can you. I mean I know nothing about these things.........
DEBBIE	I think this newsletter's wonderful Ron. So much better than photocopying. I mean I couldn't touch the paper

when you used to photocopy them.

JOE   Why's that then?

NORMAN   The chemicals in the paper,

DEBBIE   I think it was the toner actually…

NORMAN   Used to make Debbie's hands blister up. They used to look
                terrible didn't they?

DEBBIE   Ooh awful. I couldn't touch anything for days after
                handling that newsletter. But I don't get any problems with
                this computer printed stuff.

RON   Oh that's good. One satisfied customer. We aim to please.

JOAN   Ron…I'd like to order some cards.

RON   Oh yes, let's go over here and I'll write down the order.

                *(They move to one side. The others are still looking at the
                cards and the newsletters and drinking their cups of tea.
                NORMAN, ROGER and JOE are in a small group set
                apart. ROY comes in and helps himself to a cup of tea and
                joins them)*

JOE   So how's retirement for you three?

                *(ROGER and NORMAN look at each other, knowing
                what's coming.)*

ROGER   Very good. I keep myself busy you know.

NORMAN   Yep. That's the key to successful retirement – keeping
                yourself busy.

ROY   *(ironically)* Keeping busy. Oh yes. I find that going to the
                gym takes up all my time.

                (The others laugh.)

JOE	So no financial worries then?
ROGER	Not me.
NORMAN	Nope.
ROY	What do you mean?
JOE	*(Going up to ROY, putting his arm round him, leading him apart from the others and adopting his professional salesman's tone of voice – intimate, yet impersonal.)*
	I'm sure you've got a good pension Roy. I mean you were a civil servant weren't you? But you could be getting a much better return on all your investments. Can I just take a minute of your time? Just a minute, that's all it will take....
	(JOE and ROY move away and JOE appears to be talking non-stop. At some point in this one-sided conversation, he mimes asking RON for a piece of paper and a pen and begins to jot down some figures for ROY, who is looking increasingly like a caged animal. NORMAN and ROGER look on with pity.)
ROGER	He walked straight into that one.
NORMAN	Well it's getting more and more difficult to sidestep him.
ROGER	D'you know I can't abide people who flog financial services. Vultures they are. Absolute vultures.
NORMAN	Yeah. Do you remember when he went up to Gladys at her husband's funeral, handed her his card and said "When you're feeling better Gladys, give me ring and I'll sort out your finances for you."
ROGER	Oh yes I remember that! It was incredible. I also remember the time when Sharon's aunt had just died and he had

wormed out of her the day and time that the will was going to be read and she said he phoned her up half an hour after she got home to find out how much money she'd been left and ask whether he could invest it for her.

NORMAN   He ought to be bloody well locked up.

(PATSY re-appears with LINDA. It is obvious that she has been crying.)

BARBARA   Oh there you are dear. Feeling better now? Don't let them get you down.

JOAN   We're sorry love. We didn't mean to upset you.

PATSY   It's OK. I really should be more in control. *(Loudly)* I'm sorry everyone. I've calmed down now. Can we please get on with the rehearsal?

PETER   *(calling)* Actually, can you wait a minute. I need some spare hands to help me shift this line of flats forward a bit.

(JOHN, ROGER and NORMAN move up on to the stage.)

NORMAN   Which way Peter?

PETER   Well obviously away from the wall, Norman. You'll have to lift the flats up so that they're clear of the carpet and move them a bit at a time until I say stop.

JOHN   Right. Someone will have to come behind here with me and lift on the cross beam. And someone will have to stand in the archway and lift.

ROGER   Well we can't go behind there in these frocks.

JOHN   What about Ron? Here Ron, come and give us a hand!

(RON breaks off from dealing with Christmas card orders and goes towards the stage. As he passes ROY and JOE he

realises that ROY is trapped and turns back to interrupt.)

RON   Sorry to interrupt but we need all hands to the pump.

JOE   Yeah. Right.OK. I've nearly finished.

RON   I really think we're needed now.

ROY   I'm on my way. *(starting to move.)*

JOE   So what do you think Roy? Don't you think you could be getting a much better deal?

ROY   Well it's all been very interesting, Joe, and thank you but I did try to tell you in the beginning that I don't make any decisions about money, I leave all that to Barbara. Or, rather, Barbara insists that I leave it all to her.

             (ROY goes up on stage leaving JOE looking defeated. There then follows a scene where the men attempt to move the scenery forward about a foot, bearing in mind that PETER has screwed all the line of flats together rather than clamping them. PETER, meanwhile, is screwing longer battens from the tops of the flats to the wall and is expecting the men to hold the flats and move backwards and forwards according to whether the battens touch the wall or not.)

JOHN   Why didn't you cut the battens after we had moved the flats Peter? It would have been a lot easier.

PETER   Oh another critic. Suddenly everyone's a master carpenter in this group. Back an inch.

JOE   I don't think we can be that precise, Peter. Because you've screwed all the flats together there's only a certain amount of movement in the situation.

SHIRLEY   *(deciding that the situation might get difficult)* I think I'll make everyone another cuppa.

DEBBIE   I'll help you. I need to go to the kitchen to take a pill anyway.

(SHIRLEY and DEBBIE exit.)

PETER   *(testily)* Keep it up – just keep it up and you'll find that this will be the last set I build for this group. I've had other offers you know. There are plenty of other groups that need set builders.

(A mobile phone rings. DEBBIE runs in from the kitchen and gets her phone. ERIC stands up and gets his phone out again. JOE leaves the set and grabs his phone again. It is DEBBIE's call this time. ERIC sits down, JOE goes back to the set.)

DEBBIE   Oh Myra, thank God you've rung back! Can you fit me in tomorrow? *(She exits to the kitchen.)*

(SHARON comes in through the door. ROGER looks a little alarmed. NORMAN is, by this time, behind the flats and doesn't see SHARON come in.)

ROGER   *(hissing)* Norman! You've got trouble!

NORMAN   *(sticking his head round the flat)* What?

ROGER   Sharon's turned up.

NORMAN   Oh bugger! *(He hides his face behind the flat again.)*

ROGER   *(calling out loudly with false bonhomie)*

Well look who it is! It's the lovely Sharon! How are you my dear? I can't come and kiss you just at this moment because, as you can see, I'm holding up some scenery.

(Everyone turns to look at SHARON and there are various

greeting of "Hi" and "Hello".)

BARBARA   How are you? We haven't seen you since the divorce. How long is it now?

SHARON   It's been a year, Barbara.

VAL   Has it really!?

SHARON   Well, actually, it's been thirteen months since the decree nisi and ten months since the decree absolute.

BARBARA   Very quick, wasn't it?

SHARON   Yes, thank God.

BARBARA   So how are you coping dear?

SHARON   Oh I'm fine. It was the best thing I ever did, Barbara. Now I can get on with my life and I don't have to pretend any more. Things are going well at work and I've just moved into a new flat.

VAL   Oh, where's that then?

SHARON   In town.

VAL   Oh. I thought you liked it in your village.

SHARON   Well actually, I think you get more privacy in a town. Too many nosey parkers in a village.

BARBARA   Oh that's true. Everybody knows your business.

(RENEE comes over.)

RENEE   Hello there. We haven't seen you for a long time.

(BARBARA, RENEE and SHARON stay in a group on one side of the front of stage and continue the conversation in mime. JOAN comes over to join LINDA and PATSY on the other side.)

JOAN	Well this is interesting isn't it?
PATSY	What? Seeing Sharon again?
LINDA	*(to JOAN)* She doesn't know.
JOAN	You're joking! I thought everybody knew!
PATSY	What?
JOAN	Sharon is Norman's bit on the side.
PATSY	Don't be daft!
JOAN	She is.
PATSY	*(to LINDA)* Is this true?
LINDA	I'm afraid so. It's been going on since before she got her divorce from Barry.
JOAN	I can't believe you didn't know. The two of them have been at it practically every place within a thirty mile radius of here.
LINDA	Even Ron and I bumped into them at a pub one night. We'd gone there to meet some friends and there were Sharon and Norman canoodling in one corner.
JOAN	Canoodling! Oh how lovely! What a lovely word! Makes having a tawdry extra-marital affair sound almost respectable.
PATSY	Why didn't I know? I suppose it just shows how few conversations I have with people at rehearsals. I mean I didn't even know that Gladys' husband was ill until you told me he had died. And that was only because I met you in the supermarket. I never normally get a chance to talk to people at all at rehearsals.
LINDA	No, I don't suppose you do. Producers are always very busy.
JOAN	Anyway, why do you think she's turned up here?

PATSY   What? Sharon?

JOAN   No the Queen. Of course Sharon.

PATSY   I dunno. Perhaps she's going to join the group again.

JOAN   Oh God forbid. If she gets bored with Norman she might start casting her eye over other people's husbands.

LINDA   She could have Ron if she wants.

PATSY   You don't mean that. He's a little gem Ron is.

LINDA   I'd like to see how you would cope being married to the world's greatest computer nerd. Do you know we've had to do without a holiday this year because he's spent so much money on upgrading his system. And he's totally addicted to the Internet. He's set up a Ron and Linda website. He puts all our day to day gossip on there and we have e-mails from complete strangers all over the world commenting on our lives. It's horrible.

JOAN   God, no! How awful.

LINDA   I know. I live in fear that one day I'm going to wake up and find that he's put a camera at the end of our bed and people in Wyoming or Buenos Aires are going to log on and watch us get dressed every day.

PATSY   God.

             (There is a moment's silence while the three women contemplate the awfulness of this. SHARON breaks away from the other group and joins them.)

SHARON   Hi there!

PATSY   Hello Sharon. Nice to see you after so long.

JOAN   (stirring it) Have you come here this evening to see anyone in particular?

(LINDA nudges JOAN violently.)

SHARON   No. Just thought I'd come along and see the old crowd. I was at a bit of a loose end and I thought I'd come and see what was happening. I must admit, I've been so out of touch that I didn't even realise that you had a production coming up.

JOAN   *(lacking in sincerity)* Really?

SHARON   So you're still producing the shows, Patsy?

PATSY   I'm afraid so. For a minute there I was hoping that you had come along to offer your services.

JOAN   *(maliciously)* Well she has.....but not to you.

SHARON   Sorry?

JOAN   I mean, I'm sure that you just want to act, not produce. Ooh more tea!

(SHIRLEY appears bearing a tray of teacups and DEBBIE carries a plate of mince pies, which she starts to hand round.)

RENEE   Oh and mince pies as well. Are these yours, Shirley?

SHIRLEY   Yes. I've made a couple of dozen for each night and popped them in the freezer.

RENEE   Oh you are kind.

(DEBBIE takes the mince pies over to the other group. They all take one but don't eat yet – waiting for their cup of tea.)

DEBBIE   O hello Sharon. I haven't seen you for ages!

SHARON	No...you haven't been to clinic for ages. Your irritable bowel syndrome must be better then.
DEBBIE	Well, I'm having a bit of a session with it this week...but it's just the stress. Touch wood, it's not been too bad this last year. Those last lot of suppositories he told my GP to give me seem to have done the trick.
SHARON	How are all your allergies?
DEBBIE	Still the same. The eczema's not too bad but the rhinitis, asthma, migraines and skin allergies haven't improved. *(Turning her attention up to the men.)* Roger! Tell the others there are mince pies here. I'll leave them on the front of the stage.
JOAN	Aren't you having one yourself, Debbie?
LINDA	Yes, I should take one before the men eat them all.
DEBBIE	No. I don't eat pastry. My gallbladder starts playing up if I do. Patsy, am I needed for a minute?
PATSY	No, we can't do anything yet. Not until Peter's finished doing those battens.
DEBBIE	Oh right, 'cos it's time for my suppository. I won't be long. *(DEBBIE exits.)*
JOAN	Poor cow. She certainly suffers.
ERIC	Someone else is going to suffer if I don't get a mince pie.
PATSY	Oh it spoke! I didn't know you were still alive - you've been so quiet. Of course you can have a mince pie. *(She goes over to the plate, collects two mince pies and hands them over to ERIC.)* Here. Now mind your own business and stop eavesdropping.

ERIC	I'm not eavesdropping. You lot should just talk quieter.
PATSY	He's absolutely right you know. I say all sorts of things in his hearing because I forget that he's there. *(To JOAN)* Aren't you going to eat your mince pie?
JOAN	Debbie going on about her suppository has rather put me off.
SHARON	Oh that sort of thing doesn't bother me.
LINDA	Well it shouldn't – you're a nurse.
SHARON	No. I can clear up sick and eat a meat pie at the same time.
	(LINDA gags on her mince pie. PATSY and JOAN look at their mince pies in dismay.)
JOAN	I definitely think I'll give it a miss.
PATSY	Me too.

(NORMAN comes over to SHARON, who is on her own. ROGER watches them. MIME ACTION takes place amongst the others while NORMAN and SHARON talk: PATSY and JOAN go to put their mince pies back on the plate on the stage. LINDA murmurs "excuse me" and exits. Meanwhile the men have finished at the flats and have come down to the front of the stage to eat their mince pies. JOE leads ROY over to BARBARA and begins to go over the sales talk again. PATSY goes over to talk to VAL who is asking her questions and checking them off on her list that is on a clipboard. VAL brings ELLIE into their conversation and PATSY shows ELLIE where the fairies come in and out. JOAN dispenses cups of tea after SHIRLEY pours them out. JOHN exits for a fag. BARBARA is otherwise engaged so RENEE takes over

BARBARA's sewing task. RON talks to PETER and hands tools up to him.)

NORMAN   *(speaking loudly and pretending to be casual)* Hello stranger! Haven't seen you for a while!

SHARON   *(also speaking loudly)* No, well I was passing. Love the costume and make-up Norman.

NORMAN   *(realising that no-one is paying them the slightest bit of attention, leans towards her and speaks in a confidential manner.)* What the hell are you doing here?

SHARON   *(hissing back at him)* You rang me and said that you couldn't see me tonight because the rehearsal was going to run late, so I decided to come and see you.

NORMAN   You're crazy! What will people think!

SHARON   Nothing! I am a past member after all.

NORMAN   Supposing Jean comes here?

SHARON   Your wife's gone to line dancing. She won't come here. Anyway, soon it won't matter. When are you going to tell her, Norman. I've done my part – got my divorce – when are you going to leave Jean?

NORMAN   Oh don't start all that again, Sharon. I thought you were happy just having a good time?

SHARON   I've decided it's not enough.

(SHIRLEY appears at their side with the teapot and SHARON and NORMAN jump apart - almost.)

SHIRLEY   Top-up? Oh Norman you haven't got a cup.

NORMAN   Oh no, so I haven't. Follow me Shirley and we will find my cup.

(NORMAN leads SHIRLEY away, leaving SHARON on her own. RENEE has left her sewing and comes up to SHARON brandishing a newsletter.)

RENEE   Have you see our fancy newsletter, courtesy of Ron?

SHARON   Blimey, that's good isn't it?

RENEE   Come over here and look at the Christmas cards.

(She leads SHARON away to look at the cards. NORMAN comes back to the same spot and looks worried. ROGER follows him.)

ROGER   *(conspiratorially)* You're playing with fire mate.

NORMAN   What do you mean?

ROGER   Look, it's none of my business but why do you keep doing this?.

NORMAN   Speak plain English, Rog. What are you getting at?

ROGER   I think you know.

NORMAN   No. No I don't.

ROGER   Suit yourself.

(ROGER walks away, NORMAN thinks for a moment, then puts down his tea and exits. SHARON watches him go. MIME ACTION behind ROGER and VAL's conversation : LINDA comes back and talks to RON, PETER has come down the ladder for a cup of tea. JOHN has come back from having a fag and is eating a mince pie. DEBBIE has come back, without her wig, obviously with a headache and is sniffing some smelling salts.)

(VAL comes up to ROGER)

VAL   I hope you're not involved in this latest stupidity of

Norman's.

ROGER	No dear. Not at all.
VAL	Only our relationship with Jean has never recovered from his last affair when he used you as an alibi.
ROGER	I didn't know he was doing that. You know I didn't know he was doing that.
VAL	I know that – *you* know that – but *Jean* isn't sure. She's very offhand with me whenever I meet her in the town.
ROGER	She's just embarrassed because you know what Norman's like. It's nothing personal.
VAL	I just don't understand why she puts up with it.

(ROGER shrugs his shoulders and VAL turns away to talk to PATSY and ELLIE.)

VAL	I don't want to worry you but Debbie's got a headache now. I hope she's going to last out the week.
ELLIE	*(eagerly)* I could play her part if she gets ill.
PATSY	Thank you dear, but it's a very big part.
ELLIE	*(insistent)* I know all the lines.
VAL	What, all of them!
ELLIE	Yes.
PATSY	Well, that's comforting to know. I'll bear that in mind Ellie.

(PATSY and VAL get up on the stage and disappear behind the set. RENEE has stopped sewing for a moment and is having a cup of tea. BARBARA leaves ROY and walks across to the curtains on the opposite side of the stage to inspect them to see if they need repairs. She is followed by a determined JOE.)

JOE

So what do you think Barbara? Do you agree that Roy really needs a different policy and that he is not really utilising his funds to his best advantage? Do you have any questions?

BARBARA

Yes. Why don't you get a proper job and stop trying to sell insurance to all your friends?

JOE

Oh. But surely you want to see Roy get a proper return on his investments.

BARBARA

The only return I have ever been interested in was Roy returning home from work safely and handing his salary over to me.

JOE

(almost sneering) Over to you? Did you give him pocket money or something?

BARBARA

Yes Mr Financial Wizard, I did. And that's how we managed to bring up five children, have two foreign holidays a year, buy a boat and an apartment in Italy. Our house is worth three hundred thousand, we have plenty of income and we don't need any more insurance. Flippin' insurance companies! What do they know about finances. They just want to take your money and give you precious little in return. I could teach you a few things about making investments. So sod off and don't bother me any more!

(JOE looks at her for a moment and she glares at him. Realising he has lost this one, he exits. PATSY and VAL reappear from behind the set.)

PATSY

Peter, are you finished? Because I really would like to get something done. We've been here three quarters of an hour already and we haven't done a thing.

PETER	Yes. I've finished the battens. You can go ahead. Can I borrow a few of the men to bring the coach in?
PATSY	Well, I'm not sure what we're going to do about the coach...
PETER	Oh, I've got all that solved. Don't worry about that. I sorted all that out this afternoon.
PATSY	You did?
PETER	Yes. I'll show you in a minute. First we'd better get it in the hall. I can't use the blokes in frocks (*meaning NORMAN and ROGER*), it had better be Ron and John and Joe. Four of us should do it.
PATSY	Do what?
PETER	(*ignoring her*) Come on John! Ron! We're going to move the coach in here. Where's Joe?
BARBARA	He just went outside.
PETER	Oh right. We'll find him.
	(*PETER, JOHN and RON exit. NORMAN returns. He looks at SHARON but passes by her to stand with ROGER.*)
NORMAN	What's happening then?
ROGER	They've gone to get the coach.
NORMAN	Oh this should be good.
	(*The door opens and there are a few shouted instructions. RENEE and SHARON move away from the little table and go and sit on the stage. Everyone is now sitting on the front of the stage waiting.*)

PETER

Right. OK. Gently does it. John, left hand down a bit – no LEFT hand! Careful – ease it carefully.

(This manoeuvring goes on until it becomes apparent that what they are trying to coax through the doorway is rather large wooden cut-out shape of a "Cinderella-type coach" standing on the floor. It has a cut out window and a door that opens. It is painted silver, the wheels are black and the whole thing appears, from the front, to be standing on a cobbled road. The idea is that the coach is flat-on to the audience, Cinderella is supposed to open the door, step into it and her face would be visible through the cut-out window. The men give the impression that it is quite heavy. Finally they inch it through the door. Everyone scatters from the front of the stage and the men manage to slide it up on to the front of the stage. Everyone gathers round to look at it up on the stage. There is silence for a moment.)

PATSY

Yes, well, I think everyone agrees that it is magnificent, but I really don't see what we can do with it Peter. It's way too heavy for even four adults to lift on and off, let alone four young girls.

JOAN

Even assuming anyone could get it on the stage anyway, now that the archway's in a different place.

PATSY

Yes quite.

PETER

Ah well, I've sorted all that. I've come up with something which will make the magic even better. The blackout will be shorter and the transformation will be quicker.

PATSY

Go on then.

PETER

(savouring this and intending to make everyone wait for the punch line) I do understand that it is too heavy and

therefore could not be lifted on and off the stage.

PATSY	Yes. So?
PETER	Well, first of all I thought "How about if it was on the stage all the time?" and we just had to turn it round. We could paint a fireplace or something on the other side. Make it look like part of the wall of Cinderella's kitchen?
JOAN	Oh Peter, you clever thing! Then the fairies would just have to turn it round in the blackout!
PATSY	Yes, that could work.
PETER	Ah, but then I had a better idea....
RENEE	Better?
PETER	Better. See that big hook up in the ceiling?
	(Everyone looks up to the top of the ceiling behind the proscenium arch. The audience can't see it but they can.)
PATSY	I do see it, but I'm afraid to ask what it means.....
PETER	And you see that rope through it, that's tied off to the side?.....
PATSY	Yes.
PETER	Well this is what we're going to do. If you notice, there's a big metal ring on the top of the coach....
PATSY	So there is.
PETER	Well, we're going to tie the rope to the coach and I'm going to haul it up to the ceiling...
RENEE	It'll take more than one of you to haul that thing up there.
PETER	Well, alright, a couple of us...
VAL	More than two I should think.

PETER   *(getting ratty)* Three or four – what does it matter? None
             of the men are in the bit where the fairy godmother changes
             the pumpkin into a coach – we can all lend a hand, can't
             we? Well, except the two in frocks.

ROGER   No, we can't pull any ropes ' cos we might split our falsies.
             Right Norman?

NORMAN   Right, Rog.

PETER   So, there we are. Fairy Godmother waves her wand. Lights
             go out. Magical music. Coach comes down from above.

PATSY   Ok.Ok. Good idea in principle – but I can see two
             problems…..

PETER   What?

PATSY   Firstly, the audience can see the coach hanging up there
             because it is rather large and will hang well below the
             proscenium arch….

PETER   So we'll cover it up with something – make it look like a
             chandelier…..

             *(JOAN starts giggling and can't stop. She has to remove
             herself from the group because PETER is glaring at her.)*

PETER   So what's the other thing?

PATSY   Secondly, and most importantly, I am very afraid that when
             you let that thing drop in the darkness, someone will get
             badly hurt. That coach is very heavy. You could kill
             someone.

PETER   Oh don't split hairs. That's not a problem. All they've got
             to do is make sure that they flatten themselves against the
             scenery –- then they'll be well out of the way. It's not a
             problem. Trust me. I'll show you. Joe – give us a hand.

(PETER gets up on the stage, followed by JOE. PETER goes to the side of the stage and releases half of the rope from where it is tied up and attaches the end of the rope to the coach – making sure it is secure. Then he and JOE haul the coach up to the ceiling and tie it off. Everyone watches. JOAN sidles up to PATSY.)

JOAN   Now all we have to do is make it look like a chandelier. *(She gets another fit of the giggles)* I'm sorry.

PATSY   It's not funny. He just won't listen to anybody. I mean how the hell are we going to disguise that?

JOHN   We could put some of the black stuff across. Make it extra deep. The watchamacallit.....

PATSY   Washing.

JOHN   That's it. If it was about two feet deep it would probably hide the coach without cutting off all of the village rooftops.

PATSY   I suppose so. But I'm still very worried about the safety aspect.

PETER   *(coming over)* There we are. Solid as a rock and it only took two of us to get it up there.

NORMAN   *(being smutty)* You're lucky you can get it up at all at your age, Peter.

PATSY   Shut up! I am very worried about someone getting hurt.

PETER   Don't be. Look. You've got the four fairies right. They're up here. They go off and get the pumpkin and put it in the centre of the stage here. *(He moves about the stage illustrating where everyone is going to stand.)* Then the fairies need to go back to here. The fairy godmother doesn't have to stand right by the pumpkin to wave her wand. She can stand right back here. And Cinderella's nowhere near the pumpkin – she's right over there. So no-one's in the centre of the stage at all. They're all miles away from the coach.

VAL   Yes. But what if it falls over?

PETER   *(speaking as though to an idiot)* It won't fall over because we are holding it by a rope at the side of the stage. Look, let's give it a run through and stop all this debate.

VAL   Well you'd better move the stepladder Peter. Barbara....you and I had better pretend to be the fairies with Ellie.

ERIC   Told you!

VAL   Be quiet! I'll go and get the pumpkin.

PATSY   Right now, let's get this right. *(She gets up on the stage and looks nervously up at the coach hanging above her head.)* Peter, you are sure that this thing is securely tied up, aren't you? Only people do have to walk around underneath it for quite a bit before the transformation scene. Like, for the whole of Act One.

PETER   It's absolutely secure.

JOE   Yes it is Patsy. It's as solid as a rock.

PATSY   OK. Right. So, Debbie, you stay right over there stage right all the time. The fairies will come in ....oh hell............the fairies were going to come in directly upstage through the archway but the archway's in the wrong place.

PETER   *(testily)* It *is not* in the wrong place!

PATSY   Alright Peter, it's in a different place from where it was at rehearsals.

NORMAN   *(joking)* I wouldn't upset him Patsy – he's got three tons of coach dangling above your head....

PATSY   Oh give it a rest Norman. OK. So the fairies will have to appear from behind the curtain now and stay down there with Cinderella. Fairy Godmother will come in through the NEW archway, do all the chat, do the spells and flatten herself against the back flats. Got that Renee?

RENEE   Yes. But I'm not very happy about it. If that thing falls backwards, I'm the one who will be injured.

PETER   *(exasperated)* How many more times, it won't fall backwards!!

RENEE   Alright, alright. I'll give it a go.

                (VAL appears with the pumpkin, which is a real one and quite old.)

VAL   This pumpkin is getting quite soft, I hope it lasts out the week.

PATSY   Oh I should think so. Now. We'd better work out the best position to place it on the stage so that the coach hides it when it comes down. Eric? Have you got some tape?

                (ERIC holds up a roll of electrical tape. BARBARA takes it from him and hands it to PATSY. PATSY and VAL crouch on the stage, looking up at the coach and judging where to put the mark.)

PATSY   I would think about here. Right?

VAL   I should think so.

                (PATSY makes a cross with the tape and stands up.)

PATSY   Right, so if the girls bring on the pumpkin and place it there, it should be hidden by the coach. OK. Let's try it.

(PATSY comes down offstage. VAL and BARBARA take the pumpkin offstage right and stand by DEBBIE, pretending to be fairies. RENEE stands in the centre of the stage, waving her wand. PETER and JOE are offstage left ready to release the rope. Everyone else is standing in front of the stage.)

RENEE   Where do you want to go from?

PATSY   Um…Now your transformation is complete….

RENEE   Now your transformation is complete, Cinderella, and you look every inch the princess. However, a princess must arrive at the palace ball in style and for that you need a golden coach…

PETER' S
VOICE   *(interrupting)* It's silver!

RENEE   *(with a sigh)* …and for that you need a silver coach. Cinderella, do you have a pumpkin in the storeroom?

DEBBIE   Yes Fairy Godmother.

RENEE   Fairies. Fetch the pumpkin, if you please.

(VAL and ELLIE go offstage right and pick up the pumpkin and bring it on, placing it carefully on the mark.)

PATSY   *(quietly to ERIC)* Get ready….

RENEE   Harum scarum, hibbedy doo. Make this spell run straight and true..

(PATSY makes a motion with her hand, there is a magical spell making sound effect and the lights go out. Then there is a crash and a piercing scream, followed by short

hysterical screams. PETER shouts "Bloody Hell Joe!" and JOE shouts " I couldn't help it !")

PATSY   *(shouting)* Oh my God! Oh my God! Put the lights on! Put the lights on!

(The lights go back up to reveal DEBBIE who has her eyes shut and is screaming hysterically. The coach has come down from the ceiling too fast, fallen face forward and it has squashed the pumpkin, which has splattered all over DEBBIE. PETER and JOE have come onstage.)

BARBARA   *(shouting at Debbie)* It's alright Debbie! It's only pumpkin! It's just pumpkin!

(DEBBIE stops screaming and opens her eyes. She looks at her dress and puts her hand up to her face. Then she starts sobbing hysterically.)

DEBBIE   I thought it was Renee's brains! I thought Renee had been crushed! Oh my God!

VAL   *(speaking very loudly and clearly)* Have you got some of your pills with you Debbie? *(To everyone else)* She usually has some sedatives with her.

DEBBIE   In my coat. They're in my coat!

PATSY   Sharon, can you look after her medication.

SHARON   Of course. *(She grabs DEBBIE's coat and gets up on the stage)* It's alright dear – breathe slowly – breathe slowly.

PATSY   Take her to the dressing room and get her to lie down. Shirley, make her a cup of her herbal tea, will you?

(BARBARA and VAL lead DEBBIE off the back of the stage. Everyone else huddles around and looks shaken.)

PATSY   *(very angry and brisk)*

                   Right. Peter, untie that bloody rope from that coach. Turn
                   it round, so we can paint it to look like the wall. I'm going
                   down in the cellar to see if I can find some castors to put
                   on the bottom. We're going to take a fifteen minute break
                   while we make sure that Debbie doesn't have to be sent
                   home and we need to clear up all that pumpkin. Peter, I
                   don't want the set touched by anyone. Don't have any more
                   bright ideas and let's see if we can get through this evening
                   without a fatality, eh?

                   (She exits with a determined look on her face.)

JOE   *(Joking)* Ooh, she's so dominant!

EVERYONE   Shut up Joe!

                   *(They all file out of the hall, muttering and talking
                   amongst themselves, ERIC switches off the stage lights and
                   brings up the house lights and follows., The stage is
                   completely empty.)*

                   *   END OF ACT I   *

NOTE TO PRODUCER – *You may have to announce to the audience that
it is now the interval – given the realistic nature of the play – they may be
unsure as to whether it is a genuine break in proceedings!*

THE TECHNICAL REHEARSAL
ACT II

The lights go up and NORMAN enters in front of the stage followed by
SHARON. NORMAN is still in his Ugly Sister costume.

NORMAN   *(defensive)* Look. I keep telling you. I never promised to
            leave Jean. The fact that you got a divorce was beside
            the point. You were going to divorce Barry anyway.

SHARON   *(annoyed)* Oh no, no, no. It was clearly understood
            between us that we were going to set up home together.

NORMAN   *(desperate)* Well it wasn't understood by me. I've never
            mentioned such a thing. I thought it was clearly
            understood that we were just going to have a good time.

SHARON   *(bitter)* Oh you and your "good time" – that's all you
            care about isn't it?

NORMAN   *(panicking)* Keep your voice down, someone will hear
            you.

SHARON   *(getting louder)* I don't care! I've got nothing to lose. It
            doesn't matter to me.

NORMAN   *(not coping)* I can't carry on like this. I thought you
            were sensible.

SHARON   *(belligerent)* You mean you thought I was just a "good
            time" girl – to use your favourite phrase. Well, I'm sorry,
            Norman, but I have to inform you that I haven't had that
            good a time. You are not as great as you think you are.

NORMAN   Don't start getting nasty.

SHARON   *(hissing with venom)* Nasty? You haven't even seen "nasty" yet. If you don't tell Jean you are leaving tonight then I promise you I will show you just how nasty I can be.

NORMAN   I can't tell her tonight! I'm in the middle of a production here, in case you hadn't noticed!

SHARON   Either *you* tell her or *I'll* tell her.

(SHARON storms out. NORMAN looks desperate for a moment then he has an idea. As he goes to exit, MORRY and SONJA enter. Both are very brown, having just returned from holiday and they are in high spirits, MORRY is wearing a patterned jumper and beige trousers, similar to the ones that NORMAN had on earlier.)

MORRY   Hello there mate!

SONJA   Ooh look at him! What a hoot! Love the costume Norm.

NORMAN   Er, yes. You obviously had a good holiday?

MORRY   Brilliant mate, brilliant. Notice the clothes eh? The clothes? Sonja said to me "Why don't you dress a bit posh like Norman" and I said "Nah, I can't afford them cashmere jumpers and stuff". Well, there we were in Spain and blow me if they didn't have some great gear at knock-down prices. It's not exactly cashmere mind you, but it very nice for all that. Have a feel...

NORMAN   *(interrupting)* Yeah, look , I will in a minute, mate but I've got to make a phone call. Can you spare 50p?

SONJA   *(rummaging in her bag)* I've got one. Here you are.

NORMAN   Thanks. See you in a minute. *(NORMAN rushes out.)*

SONJA   Well he doesn't seem his usual self does he?

MORRY   Oh, it's probably production week nerves. Everyone gets a bit funny when there's a show on. Oh blimey! I'm not surprised! Look at all this mess!

(They look at all the squashed pumpkin on the stage.)

SONJA   *(repelled)* Oh my god, what is it?

(VAL and BARBARA appear with a bucket and wearing rubber gloves.)

VAL   Oh hello you two. Look at your tan! You must have a had a good time.

MORRY   It was wonderful Val – just wonderful.

SONJA   What *is* that stuff?

BARBARA   Pumpkin. We had an accident. It's a long story.

MORRY   Here! I've just noticed! Isn't the set....?

VAL   The wrong way round. Yes. That's a long story too.

MORRY   Oh Gawd. I don't think we should have come back love.

VAL   It's alright. It's all under control now...we think.

(PATSY enters.)

PATSY   Have you seen Sharon? Only I don't like the look of Debbie. I think Sharon should have a look at her.

BARBARA   She was around but I haven't seen her lately.

VAL   The stage will be clear in a minute if you want to make a start.

PATSY   I think we'd better. We haven't done *anything* so far. *(Realising that MORRY is there.)* Oh hello, did you have a good time?

MORRY   Brilliant. Sorry I'm late but the flight was delayed.

SONJA   We've come straight from the airport.

VAL	God – you must be tired.
MORRY	No not really. But I might feel it a bit later.
SONJA	We were partying until three in the morning.
PATSY	Oh you did have a good time then!
SONJA	Fabulous.

(*JOAN and ELLIE enter, supporting a very strange looking DEBBIE. When DEBBIE speaks it is very slurred and she doesn't seem to have control of her legs and arms.*)

JOAN   (*making a face at PATSY*) She insists on carrying on.

DEBBIE   I'm fine, I'm fine. Just get me on the stage.

(*There then follows an attempt to get DEBBIE on the stage. She tries to climb up but can't manage it. JOAN gives her a push and she still can't manage it. ELLIE and JOAN turn DEBBIE round and sit her bottom on the stage, then ELLIE lifts her legs up onto the stage but DEBBIE ends up lying flat on the stage and giggling. VAL and BARBARA try to get her up on her feet but she is too limp. Eventually, JOAN, ELLIE, BARBARA and VAL manage to get her upright and sit her in a chair. DEBBIE is still giggling as though she were drunk.*)

JOAN   (*panting slightly from the exertion and speaking to PATSY*) She's not right you know.

VAL   (*loudly to DEBBIE*) Just sit still Debbie. Don't move, there's a good girl.

DEBBIE   I'm fine – stop fussing.

(*DEBBIE sits there smiling vacantly at everyone. They all look at each other.*)

PATSY How many sedatives did she take?

JOAN Just one. Sharon wouldn't let her take any more than that.

(*All the men enter in groups – talking as they come in. JOE comes in first, with ROY. He is still trying to sell him a financial package.*)

JOE ....so basically, anyone with a stock market-linked pension such as a stakeholder pension, like yours, will be able to save into an ISA which will be able to invest in pooled savings schemes such as unit or investment trusts. They should have lower charges than pensions run by life insurers.....

BARBARA Roy ! Come away from that man! (*She gets down off the stage.*) Leave my husband alone!

(*ACTION THAT TAKES PLACE BEHIND THE NEXT CONVERSATION: BARBARA takes ROY over to one side and appears to be telling him off. JOE spots SONJA , goes over to her and appears to be asking her about their holiday. VAL and JOAN are talking to each other but occasionally pause to prop DEBBIE up who has a tendency to slump to one side. PATSY is updating MORRY on the evening's events and ELLIE is listening to them. RENEE comes in with a washing up bowl and places it on DEBBIE's lap and places DEBBIE's hands round the edge – just in case she is sick. DEBBIE looks at people and smiles a lot.*)

(*JOHN comes in with ROGER*)

ROGER	...and is it bothering you?
JOHN	What, reaching forty? Na! *(He is not very convincing.)*
ROGER	Oh it bothered me. I think getting to forty was the worst. Sixty didn't bother me, but forty did. The thing is you find that there is always that defining moment when you realise that you are not a youngster anymore.
JOHN	*(worried)* What do you mean?
ROGER	Well, you know, something you realise you can't or don't want to do anymore.
JOHN	What, like not feeling comfortable going to a disco ?
ROGER	Probably. Although, personally, I never went to discos. With me it's always been food. When I was forty I decided I just couldn't cope with strange foreign food and that really I was a plain English cooking sort of man.
JOHN	*(amazed)* So, what, you don't eat foreign food at all?
ROGER	Not if I can help it. I mean I keep trying but it just reinforces the feeling of getting older. When I was fifty I did give balsamic vinegar a go but it was too depressing. Then, now I'm sixty I made the mistake of trying couscous. That was a very defining moment. I mean, what is that all about – couscous? Have you any idea?

(ACTION TO TAKE PLACE BEHIND NEXT CONVERSATION: ROGER drifts off towards SONJA and JOE, leaving JOHN looking faintly confused. JOHN then gets up on the stage to have a look at DEBBIE. He engages in a conversation with RENEE but keeps looking at DEBBIE with a look of alarm on his face. RON comes in with ERIC. RON is holding a digital camera.)

RON	....so you see, it's got a 4.3 million pixel output resolution and a 2 inch LCD colour screen which allows you to review images instantly.
	(ERIC whistles with appreciation.)
RON	It's got an optical zoom and it records movie clips with sound on the smart media memory card.
ERIC	How much?
RON	16 megabytes.
ERIC	No, I mean dosh. How much did you pay for it?
RON	Oh, four hundred, give or take..
ERIC	That's a good price. They're five hundred in my local shop.
RON	Yes. Special deal. I'm going to transform our programmes. Patsy! *(He calls out and PATSY comes forward., ERIC goes back to the lighting table.)* If you could just call everyone together then I can take the photographs for the programme.
PATSY	What do you mean? I thought you'd done the programmes?
RON	Well, I had it ready on the computer but then I invested in this digital camera and I'm going to insert photographs of everyone in the text, like they do in the professional theatre.
PATSY	But Ron, the first performance is on Thursday. How on earth are you going to print off three hundred programmes by then?
RON	Oh a piece of cake. I've earmarked Wednesday and I

shall spend all day printing them off on the computer. Linda's going to fold them.

(LINDA enters just at this moment.)

LINDA   What's Linda going to do?

RON   Fold all the programmes dear.

LINDA   Am I? That's nice.

PATSY   That's a hell of a job for one person. We only need about eighty for the first night. Why don't you bring the rest in and we can fold them backstage while the show is on.

ELLIE   *(eagerly)* I can do that.

PATSY   You can't do everything dear. You're playing a fairy now.

ELLIE   But I'm only on in one scene. I'll have plenty of time to fold programmes.

             (At that point, no-one has been paying attention to DEBBIE, who slumps off the chair with her washing up bowl and falls on the stage, giggling. Everyone on stage rushes to help her back into the chair again. The washing up bowl is placed in her lap once more.)

PATSY   *(sighing)* You could even be playing Cinderella by the end of this evening Ellie.

             (SHARON, SHIRLEY and PETER come in through the door. PETER is carrying a hardboard shape of a fireplace, which he intends to attach to the back of the 'coach' and the ladies are carrying pots of paint and brushes.)

PATSY   Oh Sharon, thank God you're still here. There is something seriously wrong with Debbie.

SHARON   Let's have a look.

              (SHARON puts down her paint tins and gets up on the stage.)

PETER   *(his response to everything)* Shirley, make a cup of tea will you?

SHIRLEY   Righto. *(SHIRLEY exits.)*

SHARON   Debbie. Debbie. It's Sharon, can you see me? Debbie, how many fingers am I holding up?

              (SHARON holds up the index finger of both hands in front of DEBBIE's face. DEBBIE, with great effort, brings up both the index fingers of her own hands and smiles.)

DEBBIE   Two. ..Two little dickie birds sitting on a wall. One named Peter, one named Paul. Fly away Peter.....

              (As she flings her arm round to make one little "bird" fly away, she falls off the chair again. Everyone struggles to pick her up and place her back on the chair. The washing up bowl is placed on her lap and she promptly puts it on her head and starts giggling again.)

DEBBIE   *(singing)* "I'm an urban spaceman...(A mobile phone rings.)* It's mission control!

              (Everyone dives for their mobiles – ELLIE, JOE, SONJA, ERIC and SHARON. They all lift their mobiles up and it is none of theirs. They realise it is DEBBIE's mobile, ringing from her handbag where she left it, by the stage. SHARON grabs DEBBIE's bag and yanks out the mobile.)

SHARON   Hallo? Debbie's phone. Who? Oh right. Well I'm sorry
          Myra but can Debbie ring you back tomorrow, she's not
          very well at the moment. OK? Fine. Thanks.

          (SHARON puts the mobile away and discovers all the pills)

SHARON   Jesus! Look at all these bloody pills! *(She empties out about
          fifteen pill bottles and tubs onto the stage.)*

          No wonder she's as high as a kite! God knows what she's
          taken. What have we got here......antihistamine.....

JOHN   She took one of those before she left the house tonight.

SHARON   Anti- bacterial tablets, anti-depressants, anti-fungal
          tablets, sedatives, laxatives, anti-spasmodics, vitamin E,
          codeine, multivitamins, suppositories...Good God, what's
          this? ...oh, hairspray.

JOAN   *(dryly)* You'll probably find she hasn't taken any of the
          tablets, she's just been sniffing the hairspray.

BARBARA   Well, she had a sedative when she had the hysterics.

JOHN   And she had the antihistamine before that.

VAL   And she used her inhaler in the dressing room.

LINDA   And she did a suppository thing while we were having tea.

SHARON   *(firmly)* God knows what else she's taken. I think it's a
          stomach wash job. I'm going to phone for an ambulance.
          I'll do it outside. You'd better get her out of that costume,
          ready for the hospital.

VAL   Right. Joan, give us a hand.

          *(VAL takes the washing up bowl off DEBBIE's head, then
          she and JOAN grab hold of an arm each and stand
          DEBBIE up. SHARON exits with her mobile to make the*

phone call.)

JOAN	*(loudly as if to a deaf old lady)* Come on dear. Some nice men are coming to take you away.
RENEE	*(shocked)* Joan, don't be so awful!
JOAN	*(dismissively)* She'll love it. You see if she doesn't. I've always said Debbie needed a good sorting out in a hospital. It will probably be the making of her.
RENEE	I dread to think what her GP is like. Giving her all those tablets. Some of them are probably lethal if they're taken together.

(They lead her offstage with some difficulty, as space is still tight behind the flats. There is a bit of a struggle to push a limp DEBBIE through a confined space. JOAN goes first and pulls DEBBIE'S arm until she disappears behind the scenery. VAL stays at the other end to push.)

JOAN'S VOICE   Come on ! Push her through! Push her through! She'll get claustrophobia if we don't hurry!

VAL   I don't think so. I think she's gone to sleep. Listen ! *(Turning to everyone.)* Sshh! Be quiet!

(The sound of DEBBIE snoring wafts from behind the flats.)

RENEE   *(helpfully)* You could leave her wedged there until she sleeps it off.

JOAN'S VOICE   Don't be so silly! Come on round the back, Val, and we'll try and pull her through together.

(VAL comes down off the stage and exits through the door.)

PATSY	*(realising that the situation is grave)* Ellie! Where's Ellie? Oh there you are. Well, I'm taking you at your word that you know Debbie's part because it looks as though you are our only hope now.
ELLIE	*(beside herself)* Oh my God! I can't believe it! I must ring my mum!
PATSY	You'd better go and get Debbie's costume off her because your mum will have to alter it. Then come back here because I still would like to get *some* rehearsing done if possible.
	(ACTION TO TAKE PLACE BEHIND THE NEXT CONVERSATION: ELLIE exits. JOHN jumps down off the stage and goes up to ROGER, who is with ERIC, RON and MORRY, admiring RON's camera. Those who are left, huddle in small groups debating the state of DEBBIE's health, except for PATSY. SONJA, RENEE, BARBARA and ROY exit to see if the ambulance is coming.)
JOHN	I think I've just had one of those awful defining moments.
ROGER	Ah. Not couscous I hope.
JOHN	No. Worse. *(Turning from ROGER.)* Patsy?
PATSY	Yes.
JOHN	*(upset)* I can't do this.
PATSY	Pardon?
JOHN	*(slightly frantic)* I cannot play a love scene with a girl who is the same age as my son.
PATSY	Oh.

JOHN   *(insistent)* I just can't do it.

PATSY   *(trying to remain calm)* Look. I understand your embarrassment but we don't have any alternative. You are the youngest man we have, sadly. This is an emergency. You have been rehearsing the part of Prince Charming for the last three months and the audience is not going to care a anyway.

JOHN   *(resigning himself to the situation)* Ok. But I feel really bad about this. I am definitely – and there is no negotiation on this point – I am definitely not kissing her.

PATSY   Alright. I'll let you off the kiss. But you'll have to kiss her hand – and there's no negotiation over that

JOHN   OK. I'll kiss her hand. But I can't say some of the lines. I can't.

PATSY   *(exasperated)* Like what!?

JOHN   Well....there is no way I am going to stand up there and say " I have loved you all my life but I've only realised it now" to a teenager.

PATSY   But if you drop that line...

JOHN   And others...

PATSY   *(harassed)* And others? How many others?

JOHN   Well I don't know offhand. I need to look at the script.

PATSY   Look John, don't you think you are just being a bit over-sensitive ?

JOHN   *(being stubborn)* I know, but I can't help it. I'm nearly forty and I feel stupid playing Prince Charming anyway. Now that Cinderella is so young I feel even more stupid. We

either make some amendments or I walk. I can't be plainer
than that.

PATSY   (*trying to control her annoyance*) But cutting stuff out...
What about Linda? How is she going to prompt you if you
cut words out? I think you feeling embarrassed is a bit of
luxury we can't afford at the moment.

JOHN   (*belligerent*) Look. I can't help it, that's just the way it is. If
it makes things any better I'll sit down with Linda and Ellie
and sort out all the cuts. It doesn't affect anyone else, only
those two.

PATSY   (*sarcastically*) Oh why not! I've ceased to have control over
this production anyway.

(*RENEE comes through the door.*)

RENEE   Ambulance has arrived!

PATSY   I'd better go and say goodbye to Debbie. (*To JOHN*) You'd
better sort everything out with Linda and Ellie. Are these
changes going to affect Renee? Don't forget you have that
scene at the end with her and Cinderella.

(*PATSY exits.*)

RENEE   What was she talking about?

JOHN   I need to make a few cuts to my lines.

LINDA   Why?

JOHN   Because I find it too embarrassing to make love to a
teenager on stage. I'm too old. I need to modify some of the
lines now that Ellie's taken over Debbie's part. I'd better go
and find Ellie, so that we can sort this out.

(*JOHN exits.*)

RENEE	*(irritated)* Well that's just dandy isn't it? Supposing we all did that? I mean, if we're going to talk about embarrassment onstage, how about being a geriatric fairy godmother? Perhaps I should ad some lines like "You'll have to wave my wand for me Cinderella because I've got terrible arthritis in my wrist" or "Could you make the fire up a bit more dear, my back is playing me up".
LINDA	It's all because he's reached the ripe old age of forty I think. He was talking about it earlier.
RENEE	*(withering)* Oh forty. How terrible.
LINDA	*(trying to be reasonable)* Well it is terrible when you hit it, isn't it? Don't you remember? I was depressed for weeks.
RENEE	*(acid)* I've forgotten. That was two decades and two depressions ago.
	(RENEE and LINDA go into a huddle and wait for JOHN and ELLIE, meanwhile, the group of men on the other side of the stage, who have been discussing RON's digital camera, become audible.)
JOE	Of course you can e-mail the stuff you store in that camera too, can't you?
RON	Oh yes. And I downloaded some software from the internet which enables me to edit movies brilliantly.
JOE	It's amazing isn't though – that its days are numbered. The Internet. In a couple of years it will be replaced by the Grid, so they say.
RON	*(appalled)* I didn't know that! Where did you hear that?
JOE	There was an article in the paper about it. These scientists are working on something right now – some particle

physics thing – all about the secrets of the universe – and in order to be able to store and transmit all the billions of bits of data that they are going to generate, they have had to invent a better communications system and it's called The Grid. They're still developing it though. But it's going to make the Internet look pretty primitive I understand.

RON   Have you saved the article?

JOE   Yeah. Well I think so. It was only in yesterday's paper.

ROGER   How amazing. It appears that a technology that I have never come to grips with is going to disappear before I get a chance to even try it.

PETER   It can't make a door though can it?

JOE   Eh?

PETER   All this computer rubbish. It will never replace old-fashioned craftsmanship. Things that people can make with their hands. Come the next Ice Age, mate, there won't be many of us left who can survive with a set of tools and our own intelligence.

MORRY   That's true. I mean they're not training people to be master butchers anymore. I should know. If mankind was ever reduced to the mediaeval level, there won't be many of us who can cut up an animal carcass properly, that's for sure.

ROGER   I feel that I am in a unique position here in that I possess absolutely no basic skills like carpentry, butchery, fishing or what-have-you and neither am I computer literate.

RON   Well you'll be the first to die then, won't you? When the world changes one way or the other.

ROGER   Absolutely. I shall look forward to it.

JOE	Have you insured any of this computer system that you've got, Ron?
RON	Well...
ROGER	*(hastily)* I must just go and wave Debbie off, they'll probably have loaded her up by now.
MORRY	Me too.
	(MORRY and ROGER exit quickly)
PETER	*(calling out)* Shirley! Where's that tea? I must press on with that scenery!
	(PETER goes up on the stage and JOE and RON go into a huddle as JOE tries to sell RON an insurance policy. JOHN and ELLIE enter.)
JOHN	*(to LINDA and RENEE)* I've found her. She understands. It's just a few simple changes.
	(They go into a huddle. LINDA has the script and a pencil and proceeds to delete lines as suggested by JOHN. RENEE joins in.)
RENEE	I really am surprised at you John – fussing about all of this.
JOHN	*(exasperated)* Look...oh you wouldn't understand... can we just get on with this?
LINDA	Right. Which page first?
JOHN	I think it's the beginning of Act 2...about the third page in...
ELLIE	Is it page 49? The one that starts "I walk in these woods quite often and I have never met a beautiful girl like you before"?
	(The others look at her in amazement and LINDA finds the page.)

LINDA	You're absolutely right. How did you know that?
ELLIE	I learnt the whole play.
RENEE	*(envious)* Oh to be young and have a photographic memory.
	(Everyone else files in, having despatched DEBBIE off in the ambulance. There is a general hubbub as they all come in)
PATSY	*(announcing to everyone)* OK. Debbie's gone off now. The paramedics did a few tests and seemed to think that she would be OK eventually.
RENEE	Has anyone gone with her?
ROY	Oh yes. Barbara decided to go and wait there until Debbie's mum gets to the hospital. Then she's going to come back for me.
PATSY	*(pleading)* Right, so can we please, please get some rehearsing done now? Please?
LINDA	Do you want to go right through as far as you can? Only we haven't made the cuts yet.
PATSY	No. I think we'll just do selected bits. You'll have to get together tomorrow and do the cuts, if you can. Val, what do you need to do tonight?
VAL	Well, from a stage management point of view, although it's going to be difficult without Barbara to help me, I really need to go through the Ugly Sister's preparations for the Ball, the Transformation scene and the arrival at the Ball bit.
ERIC	I need to do all of those too. Well not the Ugly Sister's bit but the other two, for the lighting and sound cues.
PATSY	Right. That sounds good for me too. I definitely need to go

over the ballroom dances too. In costume. Morry, you'd better get changed because we need to see you in costume please.

MORRY   Righto. *(He exits.)*

PATSY   OK. Everyone grab a chair and let's start with the Ugly Sister's fight scene. Where's Norman?

JOAN   Do you know, I haven't seen him for ages. Has anyone else seen him?

(There is a general "no" from everyone.)

SONJA   We spoke to him when we just arrived. He borrowed 50p off me to make a phone call.

PATSY   John, go and see if he's in the gents would you?

JOHN   OK.

(JOHN exits.)

JOAN   *(mischievously)* Sharon, have *you* seen Norman?

SHARON   Me? I haven't seen him.

(JOHN comes back very quickly.)

JOHN   He's not in the gents and, I don't want to worry you, but his car's gone.

PATSY and
SHARON   *(dismayed)* What!!!

(Everyone looks at SHARON.)

PATSY   Are you sure?

JOHN   His car is the red Peugot isn't it?

ROGER   Yes.

JOHN   Well, it's not in the car park.

PATSY   What's he playing at?

ROGER   Perhaps he's popped to the garage or something.

ROY   What dressed as an Ugly Sister?

ROGER   Oh yes. I forgot we were dressed up.

PATSY   Was he upset by anything? I mean you know what
                 Norman's like. He's just walked out before when things
                 have upset him.

VAL   But not during production week. He's never walked out of
                 an important rehearsal before.

PATSY   *(despairing)* I don't believe this! What more can happen
                 tonight?

                 *(At that moment NORMAN's wife JEAN comes in,
                 carrying a pair of trousers. She looks a bit tense and
                 unsmiling.)*

JOAN   *(warning)* I think you've just found out Patsy.

                 *(There is a momentary silence whilst everyone looks at
                 JEAN and wonders what to do or say next.)*

VAL   *(being bold)* Hello Jean. Have you come to tell us where
                 Norman is?

JEAN   *(looking surprised)* I assumed he was here. He rang me and
                 left a message on the answerphone asking me to bring a
                 spare pair of trousers – something about having damaged
                 the pair he had on. Isn't he here then?

PATSY   Apparently not. We were just about to do his scene when
                 we realised we hadn't seen him for a while. His car's not in
                 the car park.

PETER   Perhaps he thought you weren't coming so he's driven home

	to get the trousers.
ROGER	That's a possibility. When and how did he damage these trousers then?
JEAN	I don't know. I know nothing more than the short message he left on the answerphone. I'd better go and ring home.
SONJA	Do you want a mobile?
JEAN	No thank you. I'll use the call box outside.
	(JEAN exits.)
JOAN	*(coming up to PATSY)* Well, it's all going to hit the fan now.
PATSY	I don't understand any of this. What is going on?
JOAN	*(stirring it and speaking loudly)* You look a bit pale Sharon. It must have been a bit of a strain coping with Debbie. Why don't you go home and put your feet up?
SHARON	No thank you. I feel fine. I have things to do, anyway.
	(MIME: Actors go into various huddles and gossip. SHARON moves away. JOAN takes PATSY to one side)
JOAN	This all seems very familiar to me, this situation.
PATSY	What?
JOAN	Well you know that this is not Norman's first fling, don't you?
PATSY	No. I didn't know he'd ever had a fling until you told me this evening.
JOAN	*(genuinely surprised)* Really? You are out of touch aren't you?

PATSY   Always.

JOAN   (*resuming her story*) Well he's done this twice before.

PATSY   Twice?

JOAN   Oh yes. There was this girl at Mossop Players – ooh –
             about ten years ago I suppose it must be now. You know,
             Roger and Norman and I used to belong to them before
             they folded. Her name was – um – Hayley. Yes, that's right,
             Hayley. Rather a stupid girl she was. Well she must have
             been – to fall for Norman's line – and she was married to a
             bloke who worked for an insurance company in town.
             Now what was his name?

PATSY   Never mind. When was the second time?

JOAN   Oh yes! That was here. Just before you joined. A girl called
             Susan. Now she wasn't married. And she was quite nice
             too. She played Dora when we did that production of
             David Copperfield....

PATSY   (*getting impatient*) And?

JOAN   Yes, well when I said this situation looked rather familiar,
             well it was because the same sort of thing happened then.

PATSY   (*getting exasperated*) What ? What happened?

JOAN   Well, I think this Susan got a bit too serious or something.
             Anyway, it obviously scared Norman, so he told Jean and
             got Jean to get rid of her. Would you believe that he told
             Jean that this Susan was sort of obsessed with him and that
             it wasn't his fault. I know Susan was ever so upset. I don't
             think Jean believed him because she tackled Roger about it.
             Norman had been using Roger as a sort of alibi, only
             Roger didn't know about it. It was all very messy...

sshh... she's coming back...

(JEAN comes back.)

JEAN He's not at home. Or at least he's not answering the phone. I've left a message so I suppose I'd better just sit and wait. *(pointedly)* Do you know where he is Roger?

VAL *(defensively)* No, Roger doesn't.

ROGER No dear. As far as I was concerned, Norman was here. But we've had a rather difficult and confusing time this evening and I haven't kept track of everyone's movements.

JEAN Hasn't the rehearsal gone well so far then?

JOAN We haven't had a rehearsal yet. First of all the set was the wrong way round....

PETER *(leaping to his own defence)* It is *not* the wrong way round as far as I'm concerned!

SHIRLEY *(entering with a tray of teacups)* Tea up!

JOAN *(emphasising it loudly to annoy Peter)* First of all the set was the wrong way round - and the fairies didn't turn up and anyway we're down to three because one of them has a broken leg – then Peter hoisted this very heavy coach up to the ceiling and when it came down in the darkness it smashed the pumpkin all over Debbie who got hysterical and thought it was Renee's brains – so she took a sedative, only it turned out she had taken a great many other tablets earlier and so she went peculiar and we had to call an ambulance and take her away. And now Norman's gone missing.

RENEE *(adding her bit)* And now Ellie's playing Cinderella and

John wants to change all the lines because he's embarrassed about the age gap....

JOHN   *(embarrassed again)* Renee!.

JOAN   Oh and don't forget Patsy's outburst!

RENEE   Yes. She got upset because we all moaned about having to have an extra rehearsal on Wednesday.

JOAN   Yes, she went outside and cried.

RENEE   Ron hasn't done the programmes yet.

RON   *(annoyed)* That isn't a problem!

JOAN   Eric's got to change all the lights round.

RENEE   And now Norman's gone missing.

JOAN   I said that.

JEAN   Quite eventful then?

RENEE   Yes.

SONJA   *(panicking suddenly)* Oh blimey. Morry! ....Where's my Morry gone?

VAL   He's getting changed into his costume Sonja. Don't worry. He hasn't disappeared too.

SONJA   *(being serious)* Well you never know. There might be some sort of Bermuda Triangle out by the toilets and Norman's been sucked into a fourth dimension by an alien force.

JEAN   *(smiling)* That would be nice.

SONJA   *(shrugging)* Oh well, never mind. I say bugger the tea. We've got something stronger in the car. Won't be a minute. *(She exits.)*

SHIRLEY   *(annoyed)* What does she mean "bugger the tea"!?

JEAN	Will it go ahead do you think? The show?
JOAN	Oh yes. It'll be alright on the night. Patsy'll pull it together.
PATSY	I can't pull it together if we don't have Norman.
JEAN	I think you'd better make contingency plans. I have a feeling – even ruling out alien abduction – that Norman may not be around.
PATSY	What do you mean?
JEAN	*(grimly)* I can't say at this point. I think you had just better make other plans.
PATSY	*(defeated)* Great. That's not very helpful Jean.
JEAN	*(sarcastically)* I'm sorry but I'm not in the business of being helpful at the moment.
	(SONJA comes struggling through the door, clutching four bottles of Spanish champagne.)
SONJA	Here we are. Get your tonsils round this lot. Absolutely guaranteed to cheer anybody up who is down in the dumps.
PATSY	Can you get me a pint glass?
	(The men all crowd around and start opening the bottles. JOE gets one open, ROGER another, PETER another and RON another.)
JOE	There we go.
PETER	Shirley! Get some glasses will you?
RENEE	I'll help you.
JOAN	Don't bother. We've got empty tea cups here.
LINDA	So we have.

(Everyone crowds round getting their teacups filled up, including a hopeful ELLIE.)

PATSY   Forget it Ellie. I'm not having another Cinderella falling off her chair and getting hospitalised.

(ELLIE looks downcast). Oh go on then. Just half a cup Roger. Just half a cup for Ellie.

ERIC   Oi! Don't forget me!

(ACTION BEHIND THE NEXT CONVERSATION; Everyone breaks up into little huddles, savouring their champagne. JOAN takes a cup over to ERIC and stands chatting to him. JOHN, ELLIE and LINDA take theirs back to the script and carry on making cuts. VAL produces a needle and thread from her pocket and starts to repair a tear in ROGER's dress. RENEE talks to PATSY about something on the stage. PETER ropes JOE, RON and ROY into opening tins of paint and starting to paint the fireplace shape a dark brown colour. SHARON stands on her own, occasionally looking at JEAN, who has sat down again. Everyone is avoiding SHARON for the moment. MORRY comes back in, dressed as The Chamberlain.)

MORRY   What's going on here then?

SONJA   Oh you didn't mind love did you? Everyone was a bit down so I got the bottles of bubbly out of the car.

MORRY   Is there any left?

SONJA   Of course!

MORRY   Well then I don't mind. Give us a cup and a cuddle, you sexy suntanned senorita.

(He gives SONJA a quick cuddle.)

SONJA	Ooh – a bottle of Spanish plonk and it brings out the animal in you!
MORRY	I don't need the plonk darlin'…
SONJA	Get off! Save it for later!
	(MORRY laughs and helps himself to a drink. SONJA takes her drink and goes over to JEAN.)
SONJA	Hello. I don't think we've met before have we? I'm Sonja, Morry's wife.
JEAN	Hello. I'm Jean and I'm Norman's wife. You've not long been in this group have you?
SONJA	No. Morry only joined for the last production. I don't think Norman was in that one. I've met him, Norman I mean, a couple of times. But I've not seen you here before. Do you get up on the stage too?
JEAN	No.
SONJA	But I'm sure I've seen you before. Did you come to the last show?
JEAN	No I didn't. Perhaps you've just seen me shopping in the town.
SONJA	Perhaps. It's a nice friendly drama group isn't it?
JEAN	Hmm. A bit too friendly sometimes.
SONJA	Oh you can't be too friendly. Do you have a hobby – like this?
JEAN	Well, I go to line dancing…
SONJA	What, that American cowboy stuff. Ooh I've always liked the look of that. Where do you go then ? To do this dancing?
JEAN	The WI hall.
SONJA	Oh I know……..Oh God! You don't belong to that class

that's run by that gorgeous Italian bloke do you? Whatsisname? Er...

JEAN   Mario. Yes I do.

SONJA   Cor! He's fabulous! My friend Paula goes there. In fact I think every woman for about forty miles around goes there. I tried to sign up but he's so popular you can't get a place for love or money.

JEAN   Yes. Mario's very good.

SONJA   Here! Now I remember where I've seen you! I saw you in that new pub place on the coast road with him the other week. I was with another friend of mine and she pointed out this gorgeous bloke on the other side of the room and said "That's the bloke who runs those line dancing classes." And you were with him. You had a really nice green dress on. Last Thursday wasn't it?

JEAN   Er, yes.....he was having a night out with a few of his students....a few of us went there.

SONJA   Oh, I didn't notice anyone else. What a guy he is. Cor, having a night out with the teacher eh? Bet you wished it was just you and him having a night out eh? I wouldn't want to share him with anybody.

JEAN   Er, would you excuse me a moment? Sorry...um...

SONJA   Sonja......

JEAN   Sorry Sonja. I just need a word with Patsy a minute.

SONJA   That's alright. I'd better go and keep an eye on Morry. He drinks that Spanish bubbly like water if he's left to it.

(They both separate. SONJA goes over to MORRY and

takes a bottle away from him. JEAN motions PATSY down off the stage.)

JEAN   I'm sorry about what I said earlier but I do think that you had better find a replacement for Norman. I'm serious about it.

PATSY   I can't do that at the eleventh hour Jean. I mean, look, *(she motions at the cast)* the only spare people I've got are women – and they haven't learnt the lines. We've got our first performance in three days time. I mean what is all this about Jean? Why are you insisting that Norman won't be available?

JEAN   I think you know as well as I do.

PATSY   I don't.

JEAN   Come on Patsy. This is very embarrassing for me.

PATSY   *(insisting)* Jean, I haven't the foggiest.

JEAN   *(being blunt)* Is it you?

PATSY   Sorry?

JEAN   Is it you that Norman is having the affair with?

PATSY   *(embarrassed)* What?! Are you mad?!

JEAN   *(remarkably composed)* Please tell me the truth.

PATSY   *(telling it like it is)* Jean, I have two children still at primary school – I'm going through the menopause – by seven o clock in the evening I'm so tired I have to take my dinner through a straw – do me a favour!

JEAN   *(determined)* I know it's someone here. He's done this to me before. He'll disappear now for about a week and he'll come back expecting me to have sent the bitch packing.

Well things aren't going to work out quite as he hopes, because I have got some plans of my own. But I just want to know who it is, that's all.

PATSY
Well don't ask me. I know nothing. Everyone will tell you that I know nothing. No-one ever tells me anything.

JEAN
(she gives up on PATSY) Right. Sorry.

(JEAN walks off and goes to get herself another drink. She stops and has takes a long hard look at SHARON as she passes. SHAARON turns her head away in embarrassment and then gets up and goes to chat to RON, ROY and JOE. PATSY motions ROGER down off the stage.)

ROGER
What is it lovely Patsy?

PATSY
We have a big problem. The worst kind of problem.

ROGER
(alarmed) Another one! What?

PATSY
Jean is quite positive that Norman will not be back for a week and we will have to replace him.

ROGER
Is this to do with…*(He makes a motion with his head towards SHARON.)*

PATSY
Apparently, but she doesn't know it's her – yet. I hope to God that Joan doesn't take it into her head to enlighten her.

ROGER
Yes. Joan may very well do that.

PATSY
Anyway. Forget about that. What are we going to do about replacing Norman? Do you think Val would do it?

ROGER
Definitely not. The part's too physical.

PATSY
That eliminates Barbara too.

ROGER
I would think so. And we don't have any spare men.

PATSY	Even if we did – no-one could learn the lines in time.
ROGER	No. Wait a minute. I've just had a thought. *I* know all of Norman's lines.
PATSY	Yes, but you can't play both parts.
ROGER	Yes I could. You remember that comedienne – what was her name – northern woman – little – had a partner who was a big tall woman who never spoke a word – um…….
PATSY	Hylda Baker?
ROGER	That's it! Hylda Baker. Now. If I had a partner like that – I could do all the lines and the other Ugly Sister could just be a dumb straight man.
PATSY	Could you do that? Really?
ROGER	I think so. I mean I could almost make it up as I go along.
PATSY	Like you do anyway dear.
ROGER	Like I do anyway.
PATSY	But who?
ROGER	Let's see. *(They both look around at the cast.)* Ron? No. He's Dandini. Too big a part.
PATSY	Joe has much too big a part as Buttons.
ROGER	Yes and anyway, he's too good in that part, you wouldn't want to waste him.
PATSY	Morry! He's only The Chamberlain. He only calls out the names of the people who come to the ball!
ROGER	Yes, that's right. Now, that's a part that Val could do. She only has to read off some cards.
PATSY	That's right. Oh God, I think we've cracked it! If you're

sure that you can do it?

ROGER   Well why don't we rehearse it now?

PATSY   I need another drink first. (*Calling*) Morry – can you come here a minute – and bring a bottle with you.

(MORRY comes over with the bottle of champagne he has retrieved from SONJA.)

PATSY   Right. Now we have to take some emergency action. Give me a drink first and we'll explain it to you.

(ACTION TO BE TAKEN BEHIND THE NEXT CONVERSATION: PATSY, ROGER and MORRY go into a huddle and MORRY is seen to be laughing and nodding. Meanwhile SONJA has been buttonholed by JOE who gets some papers out of his pocket and is trying to sell her some insurance. RON marshals one or two people onstage and starts taking photos with his digital camera.(RON needs to adlib some quiet dialogue here) He has each of them sitting in Cinderella's chair in turn – first RENEE, who does a Fairy Godmother pose with her wand, then JOHN. ELLIE goes off to get the Cinderella raggy dress on so that she can have her photo taken. VAL goes with ELLIE to help her. Then RON takes a photo of ROY, who puts his wig back on for the photo. Then RON motions JOE to stop what he is doing, and have his photo taken. While all this is going on, JOAN and LINDA come over to watch but JOAN looks at SHARON and decides to take her to one side for a chat. JEAN and SONJA continue to get quietly merry while watching the photo session. JOAN takes SHARON to one side.)

JOAN   Sharon, I hope you don't mind me saying this but I really think you should go home for your own good.

SHARON   Why?

JOAN   Because, any minute now, Jean is going to work out that it is you that Norman is having a fling with and she is going to hang, draw and quarter you. And, speaking as one who has seen Jean do this before, it is not a pretty sight.

SHARON   What do you mean "Jean has done this before"?

JOAN   *(with mock surprise)* Don't tell me you thought you were the first? My dear, this is the *third time* Norman has done this since I've known him. God knows how many times he'd done it before then.

SHARON   Third?!

JOAN   Ssh! She'll hear you. Yes, third. There was this girl called Hayley, about ten years ago and a girl called Susan about three years ago. Do you remember Susan? Very attractive girl. Played Dora in David Copperfield.

SHARON   I joined just after that play.

JOAN   Oh yes, that's right. Well Susan was very upset. Norman just disappeared – like he's done now – and the next thing we knew Jean was down here, like a bat out of hell, taking poor Susan apart in front of everyone. It was disgraceful. Apparently Norman had used Roger as an alibi and poor Roger didn't know anything about it. Jean stopped speaking to Roger and Val for such a long time and it wasn't their fault. Didn't you know that? You must have done.

SHARON   *(bitter)* No. I didn't know anything about it.

JOAN   Poor Susan. She was a nice girl too. Quite lonely. I think she'd been engaged to someone but it was broken off and she sort of got involved with Norman on the rebound, as it were. Norman seems to have a nose for women who are vulnerable.

SHARON   *(very bitter)* Yes, doesn't he.

JOAN   *(insincerely)* I hope you're not too upset dear.

SHARON   *(testily)* Well of course I'm upset Joan. I realise that I've been a complete mug. Anyone would be upset under those circumstances, don't you think?

JOAN   Yes. *(With a touch of hope)* You won't make a scene will you dear?

SHARON   I can't promise that, I'm afraid. I can't promise anything at the moment.

JOAN   *(looking pleased with herself)* Alright. I just thought you ought to know.

    (JOAN wanders off. SHARON stands rooted to the spot trying to control herself. She looks around and then helps herself to a pot of red paint on the front of the stage and a brush and exits. VAL appears with ELLIE dressed in Cinderella's rags and VAL is also carrying another costume. ELLIE goes up on stage to wait her turn to be photographed and VAL goes up to PATSY, ROGER and MORRY.)

VAL   I've just found Norman's costume stuffed down the back of a chair in the dressing room.

ROGER   Ah. So he's obviously wearing his ordinary clothes and one would deduce from that that he is not coming back, don't

	you think?
PATSY	Looks like Jean was right. Morry, you'd better go and get changed to do this scene with Roger.
ROGER	It's going to be quite messy dear.
VAL	What scene is this?
ROGER	We're basically going to do the 'Getting Ready for the Ball Scene'.
VAL	Right. So you want all the make-up stuff and the shaving foam.
ROGER	Yes.
PATSY	Right off you go. Ron will be finished in five minutes and we can do it then.

(VAL, ROGER and MORRY exit.)

RON	Put your hat on Buttons. It will look better with the hat.
JOE	Oh I hate the hat. I look a right idiot in it.
LINDA	I think it looks sweet. Anyway, Buttons is a right idiot isn't he?
JOE	I think he's fairly sad and pathetic. Why do I always get these sort of parts?
LINDA	*(sweetly)* Could it be that you are a sad and pathetic person?
JOE	*(huffily)* Thank you.
LINDA	*(shrugging)* Well, you did ask.
RON	Right. Let's have Cinderella. That's it. A nice smile now Ellie. Just one more for luck. Now. Baroness Hardup I think.
JOAN	Do you want me full on or profile?
LINDA	*(unable to resist)* How about both faces at once?

JOAN	Very funny.
LINDA	Sorry. It's been a long evening.
RON	We'd better take one of *you* Patsy.
PATSY	Oh not me, please. I hate having my photo taken. Can't we just have the actors?
ERIC	Well I will not be having my photo taken, that's for sure.
PATSY	Yes. I think just actors faces in the programme. Not the rest of us.
RON	Would someone take my photo, then?
PATSY	Eric, you'd better do this. Technology frightens me.
	(ERIC comes out from the lighting table and takes the camera. RON sits down and grins. ROGER sticks his head out from behind the set.)
ROGER	Are we ready yet?
VAL	*(entering front of stage with make-up props)* Hang on a minute, I'm all on my own at the moment. You'll have to clear the stage and let me set up the table. Ellie, we're going to do the 'Getting ready for the Ball' scene. You've got a couple of lines at the beginning of that haven't you?
ELLIE	Yes.
VAL	The Ugly Sister's ballgowns are hanging behind the sets offstage right – and that's where they will be for performances. OK?
ELLIE	Right.
VAL	Peter. You'll have to stop painting for the moment, we're going to actually rehearse.

PETER	Alright. I can't do any more anyway because my red paint has gone missing. *(Calling out)* Has anyone seen my red paint?
	(Everyone murmurs "no" and shakes their head. PETER tuts and keeps looking everywhere for it. All the cast get down from the stage and get chairs to sit and watch this bit of rehearsal from front of house. VAL and RENEE set up a small table in the centre of the stage. The table has a frilly curtain around it, which goes from table top to floor, and VAL puts all sorts of containers and bottles on the table, plus a bowl of water and a towel. It is supposed to be the Ugly Sister's dressing table. RENEE also moves the chair over to one side of the table and brings on a hat/coat stand which she puts at the back of the stage. VAL also puts a large book on the table.)
PATSY	At last. Some actual rehearsal.*(To everyone)* Morry's going to take over Norman's role. Ready Roger.
	(ROGER comes on from stage right, being very bossy, followed by MORRY who is now dressed as an Ugly Sister, in a fairly loud and long wrapover dressing gown, he also has a wig on and diamante spectacles. ELLIE, as Cinderella, brings up the rear. Throughout this scene, MORRY is completely silent.)
SONJA	*(exploding into giggles)* Oh my Gawd!
RENEE	Ssh!
ROGER	*(In his "Ugly Sister" voice)* Now – it's time for us to get ready for the Ball. There's lots to do and so little time.
ELLIE	But you've only just had breakfast.

ROGER   My dear girl, you don't realise how long it takes for ladies of fashion to get ready for a royal occasion. Anyway, it's not just my beauty preparations – it's hers. Look at her. She hasn't got a clue. *(Loudly as though to an idiot)* I say, dear, you haven't got a clue have you? *(MORRY shakes his head.)* See, I told you. She's clueless. Fashion and beauty sense are totally missing. Mind you, there's quite a few other things missing too, but we can't dwell on those, we'll be here all day. Cinderella, Fetch the new ballgowns!

(ELLIE exits backstage.)

Now. I think we'd better do your hair first, then your make-up, then get into the new frock. *(Loudly)* I said, dear, hair first, then make-up, then new frock. *(MORRY looks vacant. ROGER speaks next line to audience.)* Oh, there's no point. I'm not getting through. I don't know why I'm bothering really, but she is my sister. I can't have her embarrassing me in public. Look at it. How someone as fascinating, witty and charming as me could have a sister like that, I don't know. Some quirk of nature. Some freak of genetics. Some freaking mistake if you ask me.

(ELLIE re-appears with two revolting ballgowns in violent colours and hangs them on a coat stand.)

Oh good. Right now, push off Cinderella. I don't want you copying my beauty secrets. Off you go.

(ELLIE exits.)

Now dear. Which dress shall we put you in? The lime green and fuschia or the turquoise and orange? The lime green, I think. It matches your complexion. Speaking of which, what have you been doing to your skin? You've got so many blackheads, you look like you've been mining coal all day. We'll have to put a face pack on to open up all those pores. Sit down dear and lets get started.

(MORRY sits down and ROGER opens up a large face cream-type jar, which is filled with shaving foam and proceeds to put it all over MORRY's face, including the diamante glasses.)

There, we go. Nice and thick. Just like you dear. Ooh it smells lovely! Let me show you in the mirror. Oh wait a minute, you can't see, can you? *(He takes off the glasses and holds up a mirror. MORRY squints at the mirror short-sightedly.)* No. You still can't see can you? Wait a minute.

(ROGER dunks the glasses in a bowl of water and cleans them off, then puts them back on and holds the mirror up again.)

See? That will do wonders for your complexion. We'll leave it on for a minute. Whatever you do don't smile. Now, lets have a look at your hair. Ooh my God! This isn't hair as we know it Mr Spock. Beam it up Snotty! It's like industrial strength hemp. We'll have to do some intensive treatment on this. What does it say in my book? *(He picks up a book from the table and opens it. Then he speaks to the audience.)* Have you seen my book? It's called The Young Girl's book of Dreamy Ideas. It's got everything in here. It tells you how to make yourself beautiful, how to find a man – yes, look, there's a chapter here on Regional Pubs – how to get a man – *(He does a few bumps and grinds.)* – yes, I'm very good at that bit – and how to keep a man interested – that's the bit I have trouble with.........

JEAN   (*calling out, slightly drunk and aggressive*) Don't we all!

ROGER   (*slightly thrown off balance by this but recovering quickly*)
            Er…yes…don't we all. Now, where's that hair tonic recipe.
            Oh here we are. Now, head straight dear. First we need a
            dollop of this (*takes a large bottle of what looks like oil
            and shakes it liberally over MORRY's wig.*) then just a bit
            of this (*takes a bottle of what looks like vinegar and shakes it
            all over MORRY's wig*) then some of this (*takes what
            looks like a sprinkle of salt and sprinkles it all over*) and a
            soupçon of that (*gets a large pepper mill and grinds some
            pepper over him*) then, it says, you can add some tabasco if
            you want. Tabasco? Oops! Silly me! I turned over two
            pages at once and I've just covered your head in salad
            dressing! Oh well, never mind. Just don't go too near the
            buffet table tonight otherwise someone might shove your
            head in a bowl of lettuce. Ha, ha. Now we need to massage
            it in. (*He grabs hold of MORRY's head and pretends to
            massage his hair, which means that MORRY's body is
            rocked backwards and forwards and round and round.*)
            Good. Well that should do the trick. Now, let's get this face
            pack off. (*He gets the towel and wipes all the foam off
            MORRY's face.*) Well that's certainly cleaned your skin up.
            Now we need some make-up. Lipstick first I think. Fuschia
            to match your dress. Won't you be the belle of the ball? (*He
            gets some lipstick and draws a very large cupid-bow mouth
            over MORRY's lips and fills it in.*) Smile!

            (*MORRY obliges.*) Perfect. Now, lime green eyeshadow to
            match the rest of the dress. Close your eyes. (*MORRY
            closes his eyes and ROGER puts lime green colour from
            the eyelashes right up to each eyebrow.*) Open your eyes.

Oh Elizabeth Taylor eat your heart out. I'm so good at this I should turn professional. Now, some definition on the eyebrows.*(He gets a large black eyebrow pencil and draws some very heavy eyebrows in.)* And to finish it all off, just a touch of face powder. *(He opens up a box and gets out a very big powder puff and smacks MORRY in the face with a huge amount of powder so he looks like he's covered in flour. MORRY sneezes.)* Bless you. Right. Let's try on your dress and you can spend the rest of the day admiring yourself. *(MORRY stands up and ROGER helps him take off his dressing gown. He is wearing exotic underwear.)* You wicked girl ! Who said you could borrow my underwear! How dare you! Give it back this instant! Give it back I tell you! *(ROGER picks up the giant powder puff and begins to chase MORRY round the stage and off, calling after him all the time ' Give it back at once!" The rest of the cast burst into applause, whistling and shouting. ROGER comes back on stage looking pleased with himself. MORRY comes on stage, grinning, and comes down in front of the stage.)*

ROGER   Do you think it works alright?

PATSY   Brilliant. Just brilliant.

JEAN   *(standing up a little unsteadily)* Bloody marvellous. Who needs Norman anyway?

            (SHARON enters with the pot of red paint and puts it on the stage. JEAN spots her.)

JEAN   *(pointing at SHARON accusingly)* Except for her. She needs Norman, I bet. *(She advances on SHARON, who backs slowly up the steps onto the stage. JEAN follows her talking all the time until they are both on the stage, either side of ROGER.)* I know your game, lady. You are my husband's little bit on the side. You're the one – in fact you're part of a long line of women who have made my life hell. Aren't you?

SHARON   So what if I am? He's obviously not interested in you, otherwise he wouldn't want to mess around all the time.

JEAN   Oh you think so do you? That's what I thought for a long time too. What's the matter with *me* I thought. Why does he need other women, I thought. Must be my fault.

PATSY   Jean, don't do this.....

JEAN   Oh no. I want to have my say. I just want to correct one or two misappr....missap....I just want to put people straight.

VAL   You don't need to Jean. We all know what it's like for you.

JEAN   No. No you don't. You all think you do – but you don't. Especially not that one.*(Pointing at SHARON.)* She thinks she knows all about me see. But she only knows what Norman's told her. God knows what Norman's told her....

SHARON   He hasn't told me anything. We never discussed you.

JEAN   Oh you didn't. That's nice. Well I'm going to tell you anyway. I'm Norman's keeper. I wipe his nose, pay his bills, wipe his bottom, cook his meals and generally get rid of the unpleasant things in life that Norman doesn't like – like seeing off all the little tarts he gets tired of.

SHARON   Oi! Don't you call me a tart! I'm just as much a victim in this as you are!

JEAN   A victim! Don't make me laugh. A slag like you doesn't get victimised...

SHARON	Right, that's it…you evil witch!

SHARON   Right, that's it…you evil witch!

(SHARON makes a lunge for JEAN, who retaliates. They are trying to have a fight and grab for each others hair but ROGER is trying to separate them. ROGER's wig gets dragged off by SHARON.. They are screaming and shouting. ROGER shouts above them.)

ROGER   Stop it at once! Stop it I say! *(The two women back off glaring at each other.)* This is totally uncivilised!

JOE   I dunno. I was quite enjoying it.

VAL   Shut up!

SHARON   *(almost in tears)* Well she has no right to talk to me like that. I didn't know that Norman did this sort of thing all the time. I thought I was the only one. I thought he was going to leave her and marry me.

JEAN   Ha! He'd never leave me! That's the sad part about it. I kept hoping that he would find someone who would take him off my hands but no -- no such luck. I'm saddled with the bastard, cos' he knows when he's on to a good thing. Where else would he find a mug like me, eh? Someone who knows how to wash all his bloody cashmere jumpers, for a start. Someone who would put up with all the rest of the crap and still take him back, eh?

SHARON   *(shouting)* Well you can take him back again because I don't bloody well want him! I wouldn't have him if he was served up on a silver dish with a million dollars stuck in his mouth! Nobody treats me like that and gets away with it!

JEAN   *(shouting back)* Well I don't want him either! I've reached the end of the road as far as this part of my life is

	concerned. I've got a better offer – from someone younger and better looking and who makes me feel wanted.
SONJA	*(shrieking with glee)* She's running off with Mario! *(To JEAN)* Is it Mario...is it?
	(JEAN nods with a big grin on her face.)
SONJA	*(jumping up and down and shrieking)* Oh my god it's Mario!
PATSY	Who's Mario?
JOAN	That hunk who runs the line dancing! You must have heard of Mario surely?
PATSY	Who me?!
JOAN	Oh Patsy! I have to take you in hand. You cannot go through life missing out like this!
PATSY	Is he gorgeous, this Mario?
JEAN	Yes. He's thirty four. He's Italian and he has a body to die for. And we are leaving for the Italian Riviera tomorrow.
	(All the women cheer and scream in excitement. SONJA rushes up on stage and hugs JEAN. All the men look bewildered and huddle together in a corner by the lighting table. The women gather up on stage to congratulate JEAN.)
JOHN	*(glumly)* I think this is another defining moment. She is running away with someone who is younger than me.
PETER	*(losing patience)* Oh get over yourself lad. You're only thirty nine. Have you got my red paint?
JOHN	No.
ROY	Time to worry is when you are *fifty* and your wife runs away with a thirty five year old.

RON	An Italian? Did she say he was Italian?
JOE	She'll be sorry. Never trust Italians.
MORRY	*(Standing there in his exotic ladies' underwear with his hands on his hips.)* Sort of poncey aren't they?
	(All the men look at him in disbelief.)
	(The women become aware of the fact that SHARON has turned her back and is crying. JEAN pulls away from them and goes and puts her arm around SHARON)
JEAN	Look. I'm sorry I said all those things. I was just angry that's all. You'll get over it.
SHARON	No. No I won't. He's ruined my life.
JEAN	*(fiercely)* No he hasn't! Come on now. Norman's only made you feel a fool. You'll get over it. Look at me. He's spent twenty years making me feel a fool and I've managed to bounce back. Only just, but I've managed. Just take it as a very harsh lesson and don't mess about with anybody like Norman again. Right?
SHARON	Right. He's going to be really sorry that he ever did this to me.
JEAN	Don't waste your time thinking about revenge. It's not worth it. He's going to be in a bit if a state anyway when he finally comes back from wherever he's hidden himself. Particularly when he finds out that I've emptied our bank account.
JOAN	Oh my God Jean, you haven't!
RENEE	Are you sure that this Mario is reliable?
JEAN	Oh I shouldn't think so for one minute. But I'll have a bloody good time with him before we both get bored. Then

	I shall start a new life somewhere else.
VAL	Oh Jean, won't you be lonely?
JEAN	Are you kidding? You don't know what lonely is until you've spent twenty years married to Norman. I'm going to have a great time.
RENEE	I think you're very brave.
JEAN	Well, I must be going. I've got some packing to finish. It's a shame I won't have the pleasure of telling Norman face to face that I'm leaving but, still, you can't have everything. Take care Sharon.
SHARON	Bye.
JEAN	Bye everyone. I'll send you a postcard from Sorrento.

(JEAN exits and everyone goes "Bye" ""Take care" and "Good Luck".)

| PATSY | Right. Well that's it. Personally, I can't take any more emotional upheavals. I suggest we call it a night. How about the rest of you? |

(General murmurs of assent. Everyone in costume exits to get changed, except for MORRY who stands talking to ROGER on the stage and JOAN who hovers around hoping to speak to SHARON. VAL and RENEE start taking the props away from the table on stage. PETER starts fussing around the 'fireplace' and the pots of paint. SHIRLEY and LINDA gather up the teacups. SONJA gathers up empty wine bottles and puts them in a bag.)

| JOAN | *(to SHARON)* So what are you going to do about Norman then? |
| SHARON | I've already done something. Just wait and see. |

JOAN	(*excitedly*) Oh what? Do tell!
SHARON	You'll see. (*SHARON goes up to PATSY.*) Sorry about messing up your rehearsal.
PATSY	Oh it wasn't your fault. Well, not entirely. I can't believe what's happened tonight! Are you going to be alright?
SHARON	I expect so.
PATSY	Sharon, why don't you come back to the group? Norman won't have the brass neck to come here again and at least you know everyone.
SHARON	I'll think about it. See you soon, maybe.
PATSY	Bye.
	(*SHARON exits. MORRY goes up to SONJA.*)
MORRY	I'd better go and get changed.
SONJA	You're going to need a good scrub in the bath tonight.
MORRY	Are you offering? (*To PATSY.*) She's a great little scrubber you know.
SONJA	Get off! I dunno' where he gets his energy from!
	(*MORRY exits. ERIC comes across to PATSY.*)
ERIC	I'll come in early tomorrow night and change all the lights round. It won't take me long.
	(*PETER comes downstage.*)
PETER	No hang on mate – no need for that. Patsy - I'm not doing anything tomorrow – neither is Roger, so we're going to come down and put the set up properly.
PATSY	You mean…

PETER   Yes. We're going to put the archway over there. *(unable to completely back down)* Where I thought it should have been in the first place but you wouldn't listen to me would you? Never mind, I'll sort it all out for you. Leave it to me. *(PATSY stares at him in disbelief.)* Oh, that red paint's appeared again! Now where did that go to?

                 (There is a shout from MORRY backstage "OH MY GOD!". He comes rushing in, holding up a set of clothes on a hanger.)

MORRY   Someone's painted my clothes red – all over!

PATSY, JOAN,
PETER & VAL   *(They all look at each other and then call out)*
                 SHARON !!!!

BLACKOUT   * END OF PLAY *

FURNITURE AND PROPERTY LIST
ACT I (opening and general notes)

On stage :   A pair of stepladders

Tool box with tools

A rope needs to be tied off from the top of the stage to the side *(needed to haul the coach up)*.

Some sort of "gunge" in a bucket, hidden behind some flats so that Val can throw it over Debbie in the dark.

In front of stage: Lighting/sound table with control box

Chair for lighting/sound table

Several chairs with their backs against the front of the stage

Wire coat hanger on one of the chairs

Personal props: Patsy's bag is on a chair

Peter has a screwdriver in his hand

General: Most of the cast bring bags in which they would have scripts, spectacles etc.

Mobile phones *(cast members mentioned in the script)*

ACT I

Page 3:   Val enters with small box of props. Tubes of glitter essential.

Page 4:   Shirley enters with a cup of tea for Patsy.

Page 5:   Shirley brings in two tablets for Patsy.

John and Debbie arrive with costumes and bags.

Page 6:   Eric arrives with two bags.

Norman and Roger enter with bags.

Page 7:	Debbie enters with a wig.
Page 11:	Renee enters with a broken fairy wand.
Page 12:	Norman enters carrying his folded cashmere jumper.
Page 13:	Linda enters with a bag and a script.
Page 15:	Barbara enters with a sewing kit and the repaired wand.
Page 17:	Ellie enters carrying a bag.
Page 20:	Peter enters with an armful of pieces of wood.
Page 21:	Shirley enters with a tray of teacups and a teapot.
	Ron enters with a pile of newsletters and a bag of custom-made Christmas cards with a price list.
Page 25:	Ron produces a piece of paper and a pen from his bag.
Page 32:	Shirley enters with a tray of teacups
	Debbie enters with a plate of mince pies.
Page 34:	Val needs a clipboard and pen.
	John takes out a packet of cigarettes and a lighter and exits.
	Ron hands tools up to Peter.
Page 35:	Shirley takes teapot over to Norman and Sharon.
	Renee takes newsletter over to Sharon.
Page 36:	Debbie enters with some smelling salts.
Page 39:	The men bring the coach in.
Page 45:	Val appears with a pumpkin.
	Eric produces some electrical tape.
	Pumpkin is taken offstage right.
Page 46:	Val and Ellie bring pumpkin onstage from stage right.
	(This is where the "gunge" has to be thrown over Debbie.)
	The coach is dropped on to the stage.
Page 47:	Sharon grabs Debbie's coat from the chairs in front of the
Page 48:	The coach has to be stood up and made safe and the pumpkin removed.
	All teacups and teapot have to be taken away.

100

ACT II

**Hand mirror.

**Book.

** Bottle of "oil"

**Bottle of "vinegar"

**Salt shaker

**Large pepper mill

**Lipstick.

**Eyeshadow

**Black eyebrow pencil

**Large powder puff in container of powder

Sharon enters with pot of red paint.

All the props on stage are removed by Val and Renee.

Shirley and Linda take away the teacups.

Sonja takes away the bottles of champagne.

Morry enters with clothes on a hanger that are covered in red paint.

LIGHTING PLOT

ACT I

Page 1:	Front of house lights down to denote start of action.
	Basic lighting to front of stage as well as on stage.
Page 17:	Take lighting on stage up a level for the costume scrutiny.
Page 46:	Total blackout.
	Front of stage and stage lights back up.
Page 48:	House lights up for interval.

ACT II

Page 49:	Front of house lights down to denote start of action.
	Basic lighting for the action as before.
Page 85:	Wide spot on the Ugly Sister's action – until page 89.
Page 96:	Blackout.

EFFECTS PLOT

ACT I

Page 1:   *Opening of play mood music*

Page 18:   CUE: PATSY: …"another technical tomorrow night."

                     A mobile phone rings and then stops when JOE answers his phone.

Page 28:   CUE: PETER: …"other groups that need set builders."

                     A mobile phone rings and then stops when DEBBIE answers her phone.

Page 46:   CUE: RENEE: "Make this spell run straight and true…"

                     A magical spell SFX at the same time as a BLACKOUT. Followed by a crash and "squelch" SFX. (This is recommended in the interests of safety. Rather than let the coach crash to the stage, it can be gently lowered and tipped over, while the sound of the "accident" is reproduced.)

ACT II

Page 57:   CUE: DEBBIE: *(singing)* I'm an urban spaceman…

                     A mobile phone rings and then stops when SHARON answers DEBBIE's phone.

Page 87:   CUE: ROGER: " – how to get a man" *(he does a few bumps and grinds)*

                     Appropriate SFX. *(The Stripper, perhaps?)*

Page 88:   CUE: ROGER: "Now we need to massage it in…"

                     Appropriate SFX. (Football rattle perhaps?)To last for agreed time.

Page 89:   CUE: ROGER: "Give it back I tell you!" *(ROGER chases MORRY)*

                     Chase music to last for agreed time.

Page 96:   Close of play.

                     Mood music for curtain calls.